ESSENTIAL RHEUMATOLOGY
FOR NURSES AND THERAPISTS

ESSENTIAL RHEUMATOLOGY FOR NURSES AND THERAPISTS

Edited by **G.S. Panayi**, MD, MRCP

Senior Lecturer in Rheumatology, Guy's Hospital, London

BAILLIÈRE TINDALL · LONDON

A BAILLIÈRE TINDALL book published by
Cassell Ltd,
35 Red Lion Square, London WC1R 4SG

and at Sydney, Auckland, Toronto, Johannesburg

an affiliate of
Macmillan Publishing Co. Inc.
New York

© 1980 Baillière Tindall
a division of Cassell Ltd

First published 1980

ISBN 0 7020 0753 6

Printed in Great Britain by Spottiswoode Ballantyne Ltd.,
Colchester and London

British Library Cataloguing in Publication Data

Essential rheumatology for nurses and therapists.
  1. Rheumatism
  I. Panayi, G S
  616.7′2′0024613   RC927
  ISBN 0-7020-0753-6

List of Contributors

JANET BEARDSLEY, SRN   Nursing Sister, New Cross Hospital, Avonley Road, London SE14 5ER

JANET DOUGLAS, SROT, MBAOT   Department of Occupational Therapy, Guy's Hospital, London SE1 9RT

T. J. GIBSON, MB, MRCP   Consultant Rheumatologist, Guy's Hospital, London SE1 9RT

R. GRAHAME, MD, FRCP   Consultant Rheumatologist, Guy's Hospital, London SE1 9RT

APRIL KAY, MB   A.R.C. Epidemiology Unit, New Cross Hospital, Avonley Road, London SE14 5ER

M. LAURENCE, FRCS   Consultant Orthopaedic Surgeon, Guy's Hospital, London SE1 9RT

PAMELA MALONEY, SRP, MCSP   Department of Physiotherapy, New Cross Hospital, Avonley Road, London SE14 5ER

G. S. PANAYI, MD, MRCP   Senior Lecturer in Rheumatology, Guy's Hospital, London SE1 9RT

DILYS ROWLANDS, SRN   Nursing Sister, New Cross Hospital, Avonley Road, London SE14 5ER

Contents

Preface

Rheumatology is an important medical specialty if only because rheumatic diseases afflict many individuals and impose a considerable financial and social burden on the community. Most of the diseases are chronic conditions for which there is no specific cure. Hence their management is difficult and often controversial. There is, however, little doubt that at all stages of management a team approach is the one most likely to be successful. The team should consist of a rheumatologist, an orthopaedic surgeon, a physiotherapist, an occupational therapist and the nurse. This book emphasizes the team approach throughout; particular sections have been written by specialists practising together at Guy's Hospital and at New Cross Hospital, and I feel confident that the proper way to teach rheumatology is with this multidisciplinary emphasis. It is to be hoped that by using such an integrated approach we shall at least be talking the same language when we consult each other about the problems, medical and social, which confront our patients. This book is therefore directed at those members of the team (nurses, physiotherapists and occupational therapists) who may have little or no formal training in the medical and orthopaedic aspects of rheumatology, and indeed little knowledge of the specialty itself.

I would like to thank my colleagues for their help which has made the burden of editor easier to bear; the staff of Baillière Tindall for their patience during the preparation of the book; and Miss Patricia Hopwood for typing the manuscript.

October 1979   GABRIEL PANAYI

1

The Scope of Rheumatology

G. S. Panayi

There is much ignorance about rheumatic diseases not only amongst the public but also within the medical and para-medical professions. This chapter is intended as a general introduction to the rheumatic diseases, to be followed by more detailed discussion of individual conditions in later chapters.

Classification of the rheumatic diseases (Table 1.1)

The rheumatic diseases have a variety of causes. In some situations two or more causes may coexist in the same patient. Thus the knee joint may be affected not only by rheumatoid arthritis (an inflammatory arthritis) but also by secondary degenerative osteoarthrosis, and may even become infected. Furthermore, many of the rheumatic diseases affect not only joints, but also other tissues and organs such as the brain, the heart, the kidney and the lungs. These extra-articular manifes-tations of rheumatic disease not only cause serious ill health but may even cause death. Thus proper clinical examination of the patient at all stages of his disease is essential.

The enormity of the problem

The different forms of rheumatic diseases are the most common, crippling and painful conditions in the population. Therefore, in addition to causing pain, they interfere with the

Table 1.1. Classification of the rheumatic diseases

Inflammatory	*Soft tissue rheumatism*
Rheumatoid arthritis and its variants	Shoulder capsulitis
	Epicondylitis
Pelvospondylitides	Tenosynovitis
Systemic lupus erythematosus	Bursitis
Other connective tissue diseases	Plantar fasciitis
Degenerative	*Metabolic*
Osteoarthrosis	Gout
Spondylosis	Chondrocalcinosis
Infective	
Joints	
Intervertebral discs	
Bones	

individual's work performance and independence. Common-place tasks, such as the use of public transport and access to shops and public amenities, which the healthy take for granted, may be enormously difficult, if not impossible, for the sufferer from a rheumatic condition. Thankfully, society is now becoming aware of its responsibilities to the handicapped, whatever the cause.

Rheumatic diseases affect people of both sexes and of all ages. Their frequency increases with age. Thus 5 per cent of people between the ages of 16 and 44 years have a rheumatic disorder, increasing to 23 per cent for the ages 45 to 64, and to 41 per cent in those older than 65. In fact, it is likely that everyone will experience some type of rheumatic problem during their lifetime.

The personal cost

Over one million people lead lives impaired by rheumatic diseases. One-fifth of these are severely disabled. Arthritis is the largest single condition responsible for impairment and, although it is common at all ages, it accounts for as much as half of the disability found in the elderly. The statistics read like grim communiqués from some disastrous war: 12 per cent are unable to leave their homes, 3 per cent are confined to bed or a chair, about 17 per cent are unable to bathe themselves. The numbers of admissions to hospital and to institutions for long-term care must be added to these statistics. The figures represent personal suffering of an enormous degree, loss of economic and social independence, broken marriages, social and emotional isolation. Those working with sufferers from rheumatic diseases must remember these enormous disadvantages. Patience, understanding and the ability to listen to the problems of each patient are vital. Therefore, the practice of good rheumatology demands time and insight.

The economic cost

It has been estimated that in the United Kingdom some eight million people in one year will have some rheumatic problem. In fact this may be only the tip of a large iceberg since some estimates put this number at 20 million. About 23 per cent of all patients seen by general practitioners suffer from rheumatic diseases. Some 44 million working days are lost annually through these diseases, at a cost of over £420 000 000 in lost productivity. The true cost is much higher than this when one considers the costs of hospitalization, drugs, unemployment and social security benefits and the loss in earnings. These bare financial statistics merely re-enforce the picture of the enormous suffering caused by the rheumatic diseases.

Team approach in management

In view of the chronic nature of most rheumatic diseases and the fact that they may involve many joints and extra-articular organs, the importance of a team approach in their management seems obvious. As a rule, the physician provides the continuity in management but at different times other members of the team will become involved to a greater or lesser extent: the orthopaedic surgeon, the physiotherapist, the occupational therapist and the medical social worker. The nurse naturally becomes involved during periods of hospitalization whether for medical or surgical reasons. One way of coordinating all this activity is by the holding of regular clinical meetings. Thus combined medical and surgical clinics are now the usual practice in most rheumatology departments. For patients who present particular difficulties in management and rehabilitation a special meeting of all the members of the team may be necessary. This team approach is stressed throughout the book. It should be a reality and not merely a vague concept to which lip service is paid.

2

Anatomy and Physiology of Joints

G. S. Panayi

The human body contains a large number of joints of varying type. Joints must allow movement but must also provide stability since an unstable joint is a functionally useless joint.

Classification of joints

There are three major types of joint: fibrous, cartilaginous and synovial.

Fibrous joints. There are two varieties of fibrous joint. Sutures are only found in the skull. Syndesmoses are more common and are found elsewhere in the body. Examples include the union of the radius to the ulna, and the ligamenta flava uniting adjacent vertebrae.

Cartilaginous joints. The main type of cartilaginous joint found in adult life consists of fibrocartilage and the main examples lie between adjacent vertebrae and in the symphysis pubis.

Synovial joints. The most important joints in rheumatology are the synovial joints. The bone ends of synovial joints are covered by hyaline articular cartilage and separated by a joint cavity containing synovial fluid which is secreted by the

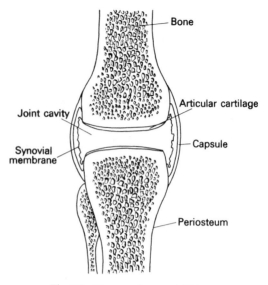

Fig. 2.1. Diagram of a synovial joint.

synovial membrane surrounding the joint (Fig. 2.1). A synovial joint is kept together primarily by the strength of the articular ligaments and the tension of surrounding muscles. The hip joint maintains stability because of the close apposition of the ball-shaped femoral head into the socket-shaped acetabulum. The particular feature of synovial joints is their large range of movement. In order to achieve this they have a variety of articular shapes, for example the ball and socket joint of the hip, the hinge joints in the fingers and the knee, and the pivot joint between the odontoid peg of the axis and the atlas which allows the head to rotate.

The anatomy of the spine

Disease of the spine is particularly common so that a knowledge of its anatomy is important. The spine in essence consists of blocks of bone—the vertebrae—joined together by synovial joints, the apophyseal joints, and the intervertebral

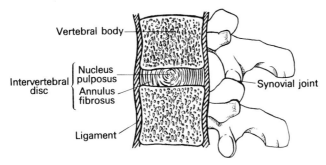

Fig. 2.2. Diagram of a vertebra showing its relationship to the disc, apophyseal joint and ligaments.

discs (Fig. 2.2). The arrangement is given additional stability by strong ligaments joining the vertebrae together. Disorders of the intervertebral disc are an important cause of human pathology. This is because Man's upright posture has imposed extra stresses and strains on these structures. The disc consists of an outer, dense and extremely strong annulus fibrosus which is composed of fibrocartilage and a central, soft, gelatinous part called the nucleus pulposus which acts as a 'shock-absorber'. With advancing age biochemical and other changes affect the disc so that it is less capable of sustaining the loads put upon it. The nucleus pulposus may then tear the annulus and prolapse through it giving rise to the symptoms commonly ascribed as being due to a 'slipped disc'.

Physiology of synovial joints

The bone ends in a synovial joint are covered by a layer of hyaline articular cartilage. This consists of cartilage cells—chondrocytes—embedded in the cartilage matrix which is secreted by the chondrocytes. Cartilage is very much alive and the chondrocytes are constantly synthesizing matrix components. The basic components of the matrix are collagen bundles and trapped between them are other materials which give cartilage its unique capacity for altering shape during joint movement. Chondrocytes are fed by the diffusion of materials from the synovial fluid through the cartilage matrix. The increase in intra-articular pressure which occurs during joint movement probably promotes this nutritional process.

Since the main function of the synovial joint is movement, lubrication is clearly very important. Living as we do in a mechanical age, we are all aware of the importance of adequate lubrication for the proper function of all moving parts whether in motor cars or in sewing machines. Two components are involved in joint lubrication: synovial fluid and articular cartilage. Synovial fluid is secreted by the synovial membrane but some components are plasma proteins which have leaked through synovial blood vessels into the joint cavity. The synovial fluid contains some very high molecular weight substances which are very efficient lubricants. One of these is hyaluronic acid, which acts very much like lubricating oil in a machine.

The second component in joint lubrication is the articular cartilage. The apposed articular cartilages have an extremely smooth surface so that movement between them is smooth and requires little energy. If any irregularity appears then excessive pressures are generated and the cartilage begins to break down. In addition, the cartilage matrix contains a lot of water. Consequently when it has to bear a load, as in the knee during walking, water is squeezed out, thereby reducing the force acting on the cartilage itself. Finally, a special film of synovial fluid lubricant forms on the surface of the articular cartilage. This film of lubricant is extremely resistant to removal so that the surface is permanently lubricated. All these mechanisms reduce friction in joints to a minimum. It is a constant complaint that advancing age brings with it 'stiff joints'. Unfortunately, we know little about the biochemical changes involved in joint ageing. Neither do we know much about the chemical and other changes which occur in the joints of patients with rheumatoid arthritis and which produce such severe, prolonged and disabling early morning joint pain and stiffness.

3

Degenerative Joint Disease

R. Grahame

Degenerative joint disease, also known as osteoarthritis or osteoarthrosis, is a common disorder caused by the disintegration of the articular cartilage in synovial joints. Although a number of diverse factors may contribute to its development, it is closely linked to the process of ageing and its prevalence sharply increases with advancing age. It is an affliction common to all vertebrates. Its prehistoric origins can be traced to the dinosaurs, and our earliest forebear, Neanderthal Man, is known to have been affected.

Prevalence

Osteoarthrosis is the most frequently encountered of all the rheumatic diseases, affecting approximately 50 per cent of all adults in the United Kingdom. Population surveys based on X-ray findings show that it is approximately equally prevalent in the two sexes, though females tend to have a larger number of joints affected. When five or more joint groups are affected the term *generalized osteoarthrosis* is used. This was found to be present in 9 per cent of males and 12 per cent of females in population samples in Leigh and Wensleydale. Over the age of 65 years the percentages were 37 and 49 respectively. There was a reduced prevalence in females before the menopause, after which time the trend was reversed. Osteoarthrosis affecting single joint groups shows, of course, a higher prevalence. In the surveys referred to, the prevalence figures for males and females were 51 and 53 per cent respectively, whilst in the over-65 age group the prevalence rate was 97 per cent in both sexes.

Types

The term *primary osteoarthrosis* is used where no identifiable pre-existing joint pathology can be established. Nevertheless, a number of important aetiological factors can be identified. In primary generalized osteoarthrosis the presence of Heberden's nodes (small bony knobs overlying the distal interphalangeal joints of the fingers) helps to delineate an important subgroup which shows a strong hereditary tendency.

Where osteoarthrosis occurs in a joint that is clearly affected by a pre-existing disease, the term *secondary osteoarthrosis* is used. Such antecedent causes include congenital deformity, fractures and previous destructive arthritis of any type.

Aetiological factors

Ageing

It will already have been apparent that ageing is the most important factor affecting the prevalence of osteoarthrosis. This disease is non-existent in childhood, rare in early adult life and only becomes a serious problem in middle age. It reaches a zenith in old age where it almost becomes the norm. Changes in the biochemical composition and the physical properties that presage the breakdown of articular cartilage may be identified in early adult life.

Trauma

A joint that is the site of a fracture or of recurrent dislocation is more likely to develop degenerative changes. Likewise, a joint that is submitted to an excessive workload is likely to become similarly affected. This is particularly seen in occupations associated with heavy manual labour. For example, miners suffer significantly more degenerative disease in the lumbar spine and knees than other workers. By the age of 50 one-third have already recognizable radiological evidence of osteoarthrosis of the knees compared with 11 per cent of dockers and light manual workers and 7 per cent of sedentary workers. Pneumatic drill operators are particularly susceptible to osteoarthrosis of the elbows. The converse is also true. Immobility protects against osteoarthrosis; Heberden's nodes do not form on paralysed hands.

Heredity

There is strong evidence that the form of generalized osteoarthrosis which is associated with Heberden's nodes has a strong hereditary basis. Relatives of affected patients show a higher prevalence than would be expected in the population as a whole. Conversely, a survey of relatives of subjects not affected by osteoarthritis showed a lower prevalence of the condition than would otherwise have been expected. The same conclusion results from twin studies, monozygous twins showing a very much higher prevalence than dizygous twins.

Ethnic factors may also be important, there being a lower prevalence of generalized osteoarthrosis in tropical and sub-tropical populations. It is difficult to exclude the possibility that environmental factors may be responsible for these differences.

Congenital factors

Congenital dysplasia of the hip results in a shallow acetabulum and may give rise to dislocation of the hip apparent at birth in gross cases. In less severe cases the condition may pass unrecognized until adult life when approximately one half of such patients develop osteoarthrosis. What is in anatomical terms the converse situation, namely an abnormally deep acetabulum (congenital protrusio acetabuli) may result in similar degenerative changes in the hip joint in later life.

Clinical features

Osteoarthrosis should be suspected in any patient of middle or advanced age who complains of pain, stiffness and deformity of joints unaccompanied by symptoms and signs of inflammation. The condition commonly affects a single joint but symmetrical involvement occurs particularly in weight-bearing joints, and in the hands. The familiar lesion is the involvement of the distal interphalangeal joint (Heberden's node) and the proximal interphalangeal joint (Bouchard's node) (Fig. 3.1). Another commonly involved joint is at the base of the thumb, the first carpometacarpal joint. It is not surprising where polyarticular involvement occurs that the patient may be

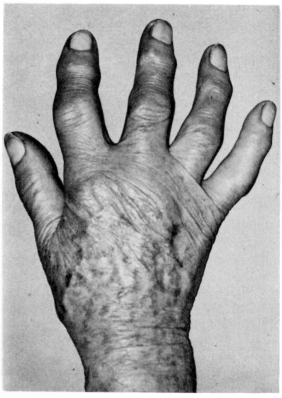

Fig. 3.1. Hand showing polyarticular osteoarthrosis with Heberden's nodes (distal interphalangeal joints) and Bouchard's nodes (proximal interphalangeal joints).

misdiagnosed as having rheumatoid arthritis. Involvement of the wrist, elbow and shoulder occur occasionally, either after a fracture that has involved the joint or in certain occupations where the joint is repeatedly traumatized (see above). Osteoarthrosis of the shoulder is much less common than capsulitis with which it is frequently confused (see Chapter 4). In the lower limbs involvement of the hip and knee is the most common manifestation of this disease. When the hip is affected the patient often walks with a painful limp and finds difficulty in negotiating stairs and getting in and out of a bath. There may also be difficulty in rising from a low chair. Examination of the hip joint in such cases reveals limitation of movement which initially affects rotation and ultimately is seen in all directions. Not infrequently shortening of the affected limb occurs, aggravating the limp. A patient with bilateral osteoarthrosis of the hips is severely disabled and tends to walk with a shuffling gait (Fig. 3.2).

Osteoarthrosis of the knees has a very high prevalence rate. In the early stages the principal symptom is pain in the knee joint, particularly on climbing stairs and on prolonged walking. At this stage palpation of the joint as it is moved passively reveals a fine crepitus. There may also be measurable quadriceps wasting. As the joint disease progresses the range of movement is diminished so that full flexion and extension are lost. The latter is particularly serious since it places the quadriceps at a disadvantage, resulting in a loss of knee stability. In fact many a patient will complain of his knee 'letting him down'. Later on, because the disease tends to affect the medial compartment to a greater extent than the lateral, a *genu varum* deformity results (Fig. 3.3). Although evidence of inflammation is absent in osteoarthrosis, the exception to this rule lies in the knee which not infrequently shows the presence of an effusion. In such cases it is believed that the inflammation is not of primary importance. It merely represents an inflammatory reaction to the detritus within the joint. The synovial fluid in such cases is of the 'non-inflammatory' variety. Thus it has a high viscosity, a low cell and protein content. There is some recent evidence that suggests inflammation in such cases occurs in response to the presence of

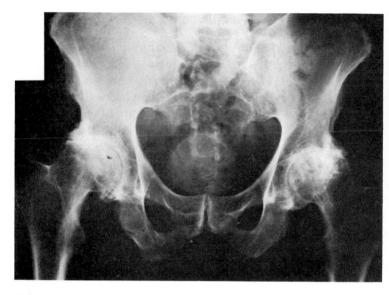

Fig. 3.2. Bilateral osteoarthrosis of the hips. Note the loss of the joint space, the deformity of the femoral head which is now flattened and mushroom-shaped, and the dense sclerotic bone on either side of the joint.

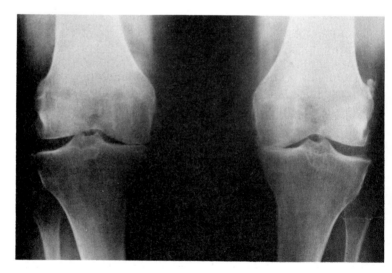

Fig. 3.3. Bilateral osteoarthrosis of the knees affecting predominantly the medial compartment resulting in a 'genu varum' deformity.

crystals of hydroxyapatite such as occurs with calcific tendonitis (see Chapter 4).

It is not unusual for a patient with osteoarthrosis of the knee with an effusion to develop a synovial cyst in the popliteal fossa, known as a 'baker's cyst'. This is often symptomless but may cause local pain behind the knee and may even compress the popliteal vein. It may even occasionally rupture and expel the fluid into the tissues of the calf producing an 'acute synovial rupture syndrome' which mimics a deep vein thrombosis.

Osteoarthrosis may occur in the ankle or tarsus but this is rare and, in the former case, usually follows a Pott's fracture. The most common site of osteoarthrosis in the body is the first metatarsophalangeal joint where it is not infrequently associated with longstanding hallux valgus.

Generalized osteoarthrosis

The term *generalized osteoarthrosis* is used when five or more joint groups become involved. It may be divided into the 'nodal' variety in which Heberden's nodes are a prominent feature and which is predominantly seen in females around the time of the menopause, and the 'non-nodal' variety, which is more common in males and occurs particularly in hyperuricaemic subjects or following an inflammatory polyarthritis of the small finger joints. Recently, a third variety occurring in males over 60 associated with hypertension and affecting the hips, knees, carpometacarpal and metacarpophalangeal joints has been described.

Degenerative disease of the spine

Cervical spine. Degenerative changes occur in the apophyseal, neurocentral and costovertebral joints of the spine in much the same way as they do in the much larger peripheral synovial joints. Here, however, the picture is complicated by the intervertebral discs which themselves undergo degenerative changes. Cervical disc degeneration shows a particularly high prevalence, especially in those of advanced age. Radiological studies have shown for instance that between the ages of 65 and

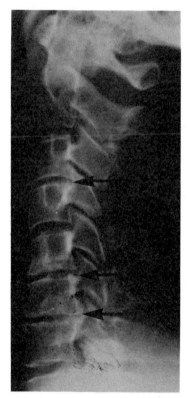 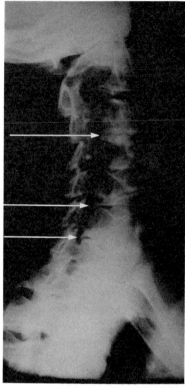

Fig. 3.4. The cervical spine. (left) Lateral view showing changes of cervical spondylosis. Note narrowing of C3/4, 5/6 and 6/7 intervertebral disc spaces (→) with osteophytes projecting backwards. (right) Oblique view showing narrowing of the foramina by osteophytes (→). Such encroachment is responsible for symptoms referred to the upper limbs.

74, 87 per cent of males and 74 per cent of females showed evidence of cervical disc degeneration (Fig. 3.4). For the lumbar spine in the same survey the figures were 60 and 40 per cent respectively over the age of 35.

Fortunately, the majority of patients who show such X-ray changes are entirely symptom-free. The term *cervical spondylosis* is used to denote any or all of the degenerative changes referred to in the last paragraph. A number of clinical syndromes have been described. These include:

1. Apophyseal joint involvement causing pain and restric-

tion of movement due to locking of these joints; this is often accompanied by reflex muscle spasm.

2. Pain, parasthesiae, numbness and perhaps even muscle wasting and weakness in the upper limbs resulting from cervical disc protrusion or foraminal encroachment of cervical roots by osteophytes.

3. Cord compression with spastic paresis and sensory loss in the lower limbs, which may be associated with autonomic dysfunction, notably paralysis of voluntary control of micturition and defaecation. This syndrome is known as cervical myelopathy and may require surgical decompression.

4. Transient brain-stem ischaemia due to vertebral artery compression by osteophytic outgrowths.

It follows that patients with cervical spondylosis may complain of a wide variety of different symptoms denoting dysfunction in the brain-stem, cervical cord or nerve roots in any combination with appropriate loss of function. It also follows that a full neurological examination is mandatory before embarking on any form of treatment, and this applies particularly in those forms of treatment which have a potential for exacerbating the situation (see below).

Dorsal spine. Degenerative changes similar to those seen in the cervical region may also occur in the dorsal spine. However, these are much less common, probably because in the dorsal spine there is less movement between vertebrae. Degenerative changes are certainly much more common in patients who have suffered pre-existing disease in the dorsal region, such as osteochondritis in adolescence (Scheurman's disease), vertebral body fracture, etc. Occasionally an acute disc prolapse may occur in the dorsal region causing radicular pain which radiates around the side of the chest, or even compression of the spinal cord.

Lumbar spine. It is the lumbar spine that provides the trunk with its considerable flexibility, but at a price! This added mobility, coupled with the load-bearing it involves, renders this part of the spine, and in particular the facetal joints and intervertebral discs of the lower lumbar region, very vulnerable to the effects of acute trauma on the one hand and chronic day-today trauma on the other. However, prolapse of the lumbar intervertebral disc is a common disorder seen in adults of both sexes and is due to the herniation of the nucleus pulposus through a tear in the annulus fibrosus of the intervertebral disc. This usually occurs in a postero-lateral direction and the herniated material commonly compresses one or more of the lumbar nerve roots causing pain or neurological dysfunction in the lower limbs. The clinical picture is variable but a common presentation is for the patient to complain of acute low back pain which may be related to a sudden and unusual activity such as heavy lifting. At the same time the patient may find that he is unable to move his back because of this pain. Shortly afterwards, the pain radiates either into the front of the thigh (known as cruralgia) or down the back of the leg (the more familiar sciatica). A common feature is that the pain is often aggravated by movement of the spine and also by coughing or sneezing which raises the intra-abdominal pressure. Associated symptoms denoting nerve root compression may be parasthesiae (tingling) or numbness in the distribution of a sensory nerve root, weakness of muscles innervated by that nerve root and a loss of the knee or ankle jerk. An important, but fortunately rare, consequence is compression of the cauda equina leading to lack of control of micturition and/or defaecation. Acute retention of urine may occur. This is a surgical emergency and must never be overlooked, if the patient is to avoid permanent and severe disability.

The problem of low back pain

Prolapsed intervertebral disc is but one of many causes of low back pain which include ligamentous injury, fracture of the pars interarticularis or the body of a vertebra, infections, tumour deposits including myeloma and secondary carcinoma, and metabolic defects such as osteomalacia or osteoporosis. Back pain is one of the scourges of modern society and it is estimated that over thirteen and a half million working days are lost per annum from this condition in the United Kingdom alone. The cost to the economy in terms of medical care, insurance benefits and loss of productivity amounts to over

£400 000 000 per year. Much of this problem can be attributed to injury sustained either at work or in the home and resulting from a faulty lifting technique, inappropriate working or sitting positions or bad posture. Clearly, much of the morbidity is eminently preventable by appropriate instruction in correct lifting techniques and general care of the back. In many patients suffering from back pain the precise source of the pain and the pathological defect involved is not clear. The principal reason for this is the very inaccessible nature of the lumbar spine and its associated muscles, ligaments, discs and joints. Nevertheless, a careful history and examination will often identify the cause of the problem and simple advice concerning the patient's lifestyle may be all that is necessary to remedy the problem.

Diagnosis of osteoarthrosis and degenerative spinal diseases

From the previous sections it will be clear that care has to be taken to distinguish degenerative joint disease from other forms of arthritis and also from infective, metabolic and neoplastic disease of the musculoskeletal system. This can only be achieved by a detailed history and careful examination of the patient, and this must include a general examination. Since degenerative diseases are not associated with any systemic upset, a normal blood count and sedimentation rate is to be expected and any deviation from the normal should alert the clinician to the possibilities of other disease processes.

Osteoarthrosis has a sufficiently characteristic appearance on X-ray to make this investigation most valuable. The changes seen include a narrowing of the joint space, a loss of the normal contour of the articulating surface and the presence of osteophytes (see Fig. 3.4). These changes may be seen in all affected joints regardless of size and situation. In the spine the intervertebral disc space is characteristically narrowed and osteophytes are seen on lateral projections both at the anterior and posterior ends of the upper and lower vertebral margins. These changes progress very slowly over a period of some years and it is not at all unusual for an acute disc prolapse to occur in the presence of normal plain X-rays. Osteoarthrosis of the facetal joints may be seen in both the cervical and lumbar regions.

Compression of the spinal cord or the nerve roots may be demonstrated by contrast radiography. This involves the intrathecal injection of a contrast medium which may be of an oily (myelogram) or watery (radiculogram) preparation. Myelography and radiculography may result in troublesome headaches and are usually only performed in patients for whom surgery is being seriously considered.

Management of osteoarthrosis

For the majority of patients osteoarthrosis is a painless condition although as it progresses the patient is likely to become aware of an increasing loss of joint or spinal movement. Many patients experience their first pain (and become aware of their condition for the first time) after a traumatic incident or after a period of unaccustomed activity. For many such patients the short-term use of a non-steroidal anti-inflammatory drug (see Chapter 11) is all that is required. Persistent symptoms may be relieved by physiotherapy including hydrotherapy (see Chapter 14).

Since the cause of osteoarthrosis is not known there is at present no prospect of eradicating the disease or even of halting its progress. However, the patient is advised to avoid excessive use of the arthrotic joint, at the same time maintaining as near normal function as is possible. This is often difficult in the presence of pain and many treatments used permit the patient to overcome this inhibiting factor. Thus hydrotherapy is a useful means of initiating exercise by overcoming pain. The use of other forms of heat (radiant heat and shortwave diathermy) similarly enable the patient to take part in an exercise programme. The exercises themselves are given to encourage joint mobility and to restore as much lost movement as possible, at the same time helping to restore muscle function where this has been impaired by the immobility imposed by the joint disease.

Acute low back pain due to a prolapsed intervertebral disc is best treated by a period of bed rest on a firm mattress, or with a board underneath a soft mattress. On this regime the majority of patients will enjoy a satisfactory recovery over the course of a week or so. Where this fails to achieve the desired effect, epidural steroid injections may be given or alternatively, continuous pelvic traction may be applied whilst the patient remains in bed.

Low back pain due to a less acute disc lesion or due to other causes may be treated on an outpatient basis by a variety of physiotherapeutic techniques including exercises, mobilization and manipulation procedures or a surgical corset.

Surgical intervention is indicated where spinal cord or nerve root compression has failed to respond to conservative measures and in some cases where intractable pain is the principal problem. Most surgeons will insist on a trial of conservative treatment before embarking on surgical intervention. The operations most commonly used are laminectomy for decompression of the cord or nerve root and fusion where instability of the vertebral column is thought to be the main problem.

Cervical spondylosis is treated with a cervical collar or traction where no root compression is present; by active exercises, mobilization and even manipulation where neurological abnormalities are absent and facetal joint locking is the problem; and with surgery where cord compression is apparent.

4

Soft Tissue Rheumatism

R. Grahame

Hench once described rheumatism as 'pain within five miles of a joint'! His unconventional definition serves to emphasize the fact that many rheumatic complaints do not arise from disorders of the joints themselves, but from adjacent structures. These include the bones, ligaments, tendons, muscles, tendon sheaths, bursae, nerves and even the overlying skin. The term *soft tissue rheumatism* is here used to denote a number of common conditions which arise in these para-articular structures. They constitute an important group of conditions since they cause pain and inconvenience to large numbers of patients, yet they are by and large either amenable to treatment or are self-limiting conditions. They are not infrequently incorrectly diagnosed as arthritic disorders and the patient may thus be given inappropriate and unhelpful treatment. For convenience they may be divided into five main categories:

1. Enthesopathies
2. Periarthritis
3. Entrapment neuropathy
4. Bursitis
5. Tenosynovitis

Enthesopathies

Enthesopathies may be either acute traumatic episodes or chronic overuse injuries affecting certain vulnerable sites of attachment of either ligaments, tendons or fascial bands. Whereas these lesions might heal rapidly at other sites, here healing is delayed because of the functional liabilities of the parts concerned, and a chronic inflammatory reaction results. Commonly seen examples of this entity include tennis elbow (lateral epicondylitis) which occurs at the point of insertion of the common extensor origin at the elbow, and golfer's elbow (medial epicondylitis) which is the identical lesion affecting the common flexor origin. Both these conditions cause pain in the respective groups of proximal forearm muscles when these are activated, e.g. as in gripping. They may be easily recognized by the finding of localized tenderness over the tendon insertion points in the presence of a normal range of elbow movement.

Another common example is plantar fasciitis, where the lesion occurs at the insertion of the plantar fascia onto the calcaneum. The presenting complaint is one of pain under the heel which the patient experiences on walking. Examination reveals a localized area of tenderness at the site of the insertion but generally there are no other clinical abnormalities. X-ray,

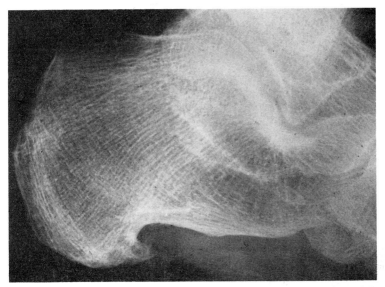

Fig. 4.1. Lateral radiograph of the heel showing a large calcaneal spur. This patient suffered from plantar fasciitis.

however, often shows a characteristic bony spur at the site of the insertion (Fig. 4.1). Although usually an isolated affair, plantar fasciitis is sometimes seen in the seronegative arthropathies (see Chapter 6). Similar tendon insertional lesions are seen at various points around the pelvis, particularly in ballet dancers and occasionally in athletes. The specific tendon involved depends upon the nature of the activity and the injury incurred but lesions of the hamstrings and adductors of the thigh are particularly common.

Ligamentous injuries occur in a variety of situations in everyday life. Examples include the sprained ankle caused by tripping, the medial ligament tear seen so commonly in footballers' knees, the whiplash injury of the neck seen in car accidents and (presumably) many incidents of low back pain incurred as the result of imprudent lifting. All these conditions are liable to become chronic if appropriate measures are not taken at an early stage following the injury.

Periarthritis

Periarthritis, which includes capsulitis, tendonitis and peritendonitis is almost exclusively encountered around the shoulder joint, which being a very shallow ball and socket relies very much for its stability on the enshrouding complex of muscles, tendons and capsule, known as the rotator cuff. It is not surprising, therefore, that trauma (both direct and indirect), excessive use or prolonged immobility or even paralysis of the upper limb may upset the delicate mechanism of the shoulder. Authorities differ on the precise details of the pathophysiology of these disorders.

Tendonitis

Tendonitis usually involves the supraspinatus, infraspinatus, subscapularis or the long head of biceps tendons. It is usually identified by a 'painful arc' of movement when the affected muscle is activated, and confirmed when pain is elicited on resisted movement of that muscle. These lesions, of which supraspinatus tendonitis is by far the most common, are usually the result of excessive use or acute trauma.

Subacromial bursitis

Subacromial bursitis is often associated with degenerative changes that occur within the acromioclavicular joint. Tenderness is often elicited over the site of the bursa and characteristically pain is felt on passive rotation of the abducted humerus. This is usually a chronic condition which may be precipitated by unaccustomed intense shoulder activity such as occurs in amateur house-decorating.

Acute calcific bursitis or tendonitis

Acute calcific bursitis is a very acute condition which causes intense pain in the shoulder with marked muscular spasm causing gross limitation of movement. It is due primarily to the deposition of crystals of hydroxyapatite within the tendon or bursa and it is believed that the acute episode results from rupture of such a focus of crystalline material into the bursa causing a brisk inflammatory reaction. The acuteness is reminiscent of gout, a condition that rarely affects the shoulder joint! An X-ray of the shoulder region usually demonstrates the presence of calcified material in the soft tissues (Fig. 4.2). Aspiration of the affected part may reveal crystals of hydroxyapatite. Like other forms of crystal deposition disease, the acute attack is self-limiting and settles spontaneously or in response to anti-inflammatory drugs within a few days. It is not unusual for subsequent X-rays to show that the deposits of calcified material have disappeared, although the mechanism by which this is brought about is not known.

Adhesive capsulitis

Adhesive capsulitis is the familiar 'frozen shoulder'. It may occur either spontaneously or as a result of trauma or in the wake of any painful condition of the upper fore-quadrant of the body which results in a period of immobility of the arm. It

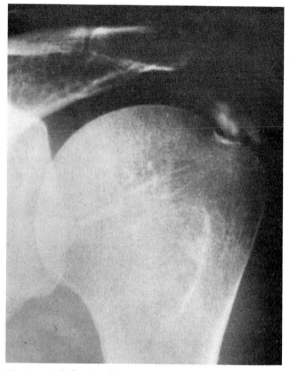

Fig. 4.2. Calcification of the supraspinatus tendon in the shoulder.

is commonly seen after pneumonia and pleurisy, myocardial infarction and hemiplegia. It may be bilateral. The degree of pain is variable but the loss of movement is a constant feature. The patient finds that he or she is unable to elevate the arm and this seriously interferes with dressing, shaving, combing hair, etc. Examination reveals a concentric loss of passive movement of the shoulder which may be, on occasions, almost complete. X-rays are usually unhelpful but serve to distinguish the condition from other diseases that might mimic it, for example, rheumatoid arthritis or malignant deposits in adjacent bones.

An extension of this condition is known as 'the shoulder–hand syndrome'. In this condition the hand becomes diffusely swollen and tender, and its sensation may be impaired. As time goes by the swelling diminishes but there is a progressive atrophy of muscle, skin and bone with attendant serious loss of function. Contractures occur and if unchecked the hand may become quite useless. X-rays show patchy osteoporosis of the bones of the hand. The mechanism for the development of the shoulder–hand syndrome is believed to be a reflex action affecting the autonomic nerves which control the muscular tone of small arteries. It is believed that this reflex activity comes about in response to the pain emanating from the adhesive capsulitis. There is some suggestion that drugs, including phenobarbitone and the antituberculous drugs, may play a part in the causation of this syndrome although the mechanism for this is not clear.

Tendonitis at other sites

Inflammation of tendons may occur at sites other than around the shoulder joint. A common example is that seen in the tendo Achillis particularly when subjected to over-use or abuse as occurs in athletes pursuing an inappropriate training programme.

Entrapment neuropathy

The course of peripheral nerves sometimes leads them into anatomical situations where they are likely to suffer the effects of compression. The compressive agent may be a bony outgrowth, a swollen joint or a tight fascial band.

Sometimes extrinsic pressure may be the cause in the absence of any disordered anatomy. Examples in the upper limb include compression of the first thoracic root by a cervical rib; compression of the radial nerve in the axilla as in 'Saturday night palsy'; compression of the ulnar nerve by swelling of the elbow joint in rheumatoid arthritis; compression of the median nerve by the flexor retinaculum in the carpal tunnel syndrome; compression of the anterior interosseus by a fibrous band in the upper forearm; and compression of the deep branch of the ulnar nerve in the wrist due to a ganglion. Examples in the lower limb include compression of the lateral cutaneous nerve of the thigh by the inguinal ligament in the condition known as meralgia parasthetica; involvement of the peroneal nerve by pressure on the neck of the fibula; or involvement of the posterior tibial nerve in the tarsal tunnel syndrome.

Predisposing factors in entrapment neuropathy include rheumatoid arthritis, vasculitis as in polyarteritis nodosa or rheumatoid arthritis, trauma or pressure, diabetes mellitus, myxoedema and acromegaly.

By far the most common in this category is the median nerve compression in the carpal tunnel syndrome which is particularly frequent in women entering middle age. The usual presenting symptom is pain and/or parasthesiae or numbness in the thumb and radial three and a half fingers, i.e. the cutaneous distribution of the median nerve. The pain is often

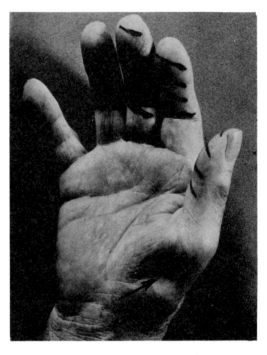

Fig. 4.3. The hand of a patient suffering from carpal tunnel syndrome. The black lines denote the area of sensory impairment which affected the thumb, index and middle fingers. Note the marked wasting of the thenar muscles (→).

severe at night and causes sleep disturbance. The patient not infrequently reports that the symptoms are relieved by hanging the affected arm over the side of the bed. As the condition becomes more marked the symptoms tend to become more troublesome; loss of feeling of the affected areas is reported and the muscles innervated by the median nerve, notably those of the thenar eminence of the thumb, may be weakened and wasted (Fig. 4.3). Carpal tunnel syndrome is not infrequently a presenting or early feature of rheumatoid arthritis but is also seen in myxoedema although usually it occurs in the absence of any associated disease.

Bursitis

The bursae of the body are developed at sites where friction takes place between bone and overlying soft tissues. It is not surprising that excessive friction may occasionally give rise to inflammatory changes, known as bursitis. Commonly affected sites include the olecranon at the point of the elbow, in the gluteal region in relation to the greater trochanter (trochanteric bursitis), in the ischial region (ischial bursitis or 'weaver's bottom'), prepatella bursitis ('housemaid's knee') and in relation to the tendo Achillis ('pre-Achilles bursitis'). Inflamed bursae not infrequently develop bursal effusions with the collection of inflammatory exudate. This is commonly seen in olecranon bursitis where fluid-filled sacs appear over the site of the bursa. Bursae are lined by synovial membrane and thus are prey to all synovial inflammatory diseases.

Tenosynovitis

Tendon sheaths are also lined by synovial membrane and are thus also vulnerable to inflammatory disease of synovium, so that tendon sheath effusions are commonly seen in rheumatoid disease, psoriatic arthritis, gout and other conditions. They may also be involved in infective conditions including gonococcal infection and tuberculosis. Non-inflammatory tenosynovitis may occur in conditions of over-use particularly involving the long flexor tendons of the fingers or the extensor and abductor tendons in the thumb. Not only is movement painful in these conditions but there is also a tendency for blocking of movement to occur with resultant 'triggering'. This condition is sometimes referred to as stenosing tenovaginitis or 'De Quervain's disease'.

Treatment of soft tissue rheumatism

Many of the conditions listed in this chapter are eminently capable of relief by local injections of corticosteroid. In others, various physiotherapy techniques may be more suitable or may be employed as an adjunct to treatment. In yet others surgical treatment may bring speedy relief when conservative measures have failed. Drugs have little part to play except as a form of symptomatic treatment, i.e. relief of pain. By and large, however, pain relief is much more effectively achieved by local measures.

Local steroid injections

As with intra-articular steroid injections, soft tissue injections are not undertaken lightly and never before an accurate clinical diagnosis has been made. Careful aseptic precautions are used and in this respect attention to detail is of paramount importance. This is the treatment of choice in conditions such as tennis and golfer's elbow, plantar fasciitis, adhesive capsulitis, periarticular tendonitis and acute calcific inflammation around the shoulder joint and unremitting traumatic bursitis or tenosynovitis. Local steroid injections are also helpful in the treatment of torn ligaments and tendon attachment tears where these are accessible.

Physiotherapy

Physiotherapy is helpful in restoring function where this has been restricted as a result of the condition in question.

Applications of heat are in themselves of little value but do serve to relieve pain and spasm and thereby facilitate restoration of movement and activity. Ultrasound treatment has been shown experimentally to promote healing and is widely used in the treatment of soft tissue lesions as an alternative to local injections of steroid.

Surgery

Surgery is used where other methods have failed. It is of value in the treatment of intractable tennis elbow. It is the treatment of choice in carpal tunnel syndrome that has not been relieved by local steroid injection; it is occasionally indicated in severe rotator cuff lesions of the shoulder.

5

Rheumatoid Arthritis

G. S. Panayi

Rheumatoid arthritis (RA) is an inflammatory disease of the synovial joints of the body. It is a symmetrical polyarthritis involving the small joints of the hands and feet in the early stages, usually spreading to involve other joints later. It is a chronic disease characterized by relapses and remissions. Involved joints are damaged with resultant deformity and loss of function.

Its prevalence in the population is about 2 per cent in men and 5 per cent in women. The reason for its predilection for women, which also applies to the other connective tissue diseases, is not known. It therefore afflicts some 1 500 000 people in the United Kingdom. This is a large burden, both socioeconomically and in terms of personal suffering. The commonest age of onset is during the third and fourth decades of life. There is a genetic influence in the development of the disease in that it is more prevalent in first degree relatives but the hereditary load is small.

The cause of RA is unknown. Infection is one of the more attractive theories but an extensive search has failed to show any bacteria, mycoplasma or viruses in the joints. Auto-immunity may cause or at least contribute to the chronicity of the disease (see below).

Clinical features

The disease may start either insidiously or acutely. Insidious onset is characterized by loss of appetite and weight, anaemia,

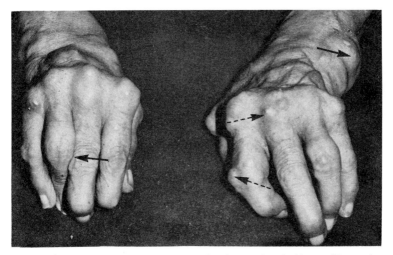

Fig. 5.1. The hands in advanced rheumatoid arthritis. There is joint swelling at the wrists and small joints of the hands [↙] with deformities of the fingers and ulnar deviation. Small nodules are also present [↗].

and pain and stiffness in joints, especially marked in the mornings on awakening. Later, progressively more and more joints may be involved with inflammation, swelling and loss of function. Acute onset is marked by multiple joint involvement from the beginning leading rapidly to loss of function. The constitutional symptoms may also be present. Fever is rare but other systemic manifestations may be found: generalized sweating, liver palms (palmar erythema), a dusky discoloration of the skin over the metacarpophalangeal and interphalangeal joints, and anaemia.

The joints are swollen and acutely inflamed (Fig. 5.1). The swelling is due to hypertrophy of the synovial membrane but effusions are common, especially in the larger joints such as the knees. Sometimes the distinction between joint swelling caused by swelling of soft tissues or by fluid can only be made after needle aspiration of the joint. The signs of inflammation are joint swelling, warmth of the joint and pain on movement. The pain and stiffness on awakening, so characteristically described by patients, is found mainly in inflammatory joint disease. It may last for several hours and be so severe as to prevent the individual from going to work.

The distribution of joint involvement is of interest. In the early stages it involves mainly the small joints of the hands and feet and the wrists. The distal interphalangeal joints of the hands and feet are uncommonly involved. The particular distribution may be determined by local factors. Thus the earliest radiological changes may be in the feet, no doubt related to their weight-bearing role, and in the dominant hand. A paralysed limb is 'protected' from the development of RA if this starts after the paralysis. Conversely, if paralysis super-venes after the onset of RA then the manifestations of the disease may decrease or disappear in the paralysed limb. This

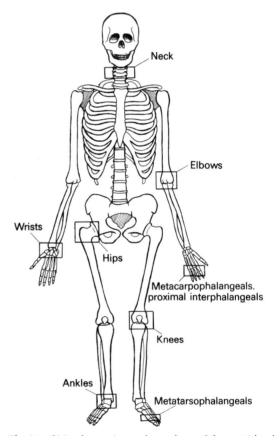

Fig. 5.2. The sites of joint damage in an advanced case of rheumatoid arthritis.

sparing effect of immobility is the rational basis for the use of splints in the control of joint inflammation. With the passage of time, however, more and more joints become involved (Fig. 5.2). Some joints, because of their situation, remain clinically silent. This is especially true of the synovial joints of the thoracic and lumbar spines. The synovial joints of the cervical spine are frequently involved and cause pain and restriction of neck movement. Disturbances of the anatomy of the neck may have neurological consequences including sudden death. Involvement of the shoulders and elbows, alone or in combination, may so interfere with movement as to hinder the performance of many essential daily tasks, such as combing the hair, shaving, feeding and personal hygiene. The loss of independence that this entails is a step on the road to chronic invalidism. A further step on this road is provided by the involvement of the larger weight-bearing joints, the hips and knees, so that walking becomes increasingly difficult.

Joint swelling and destruction of bone, cartilage and tendons lead to the development of joint subluxation with deformity. Some of these deformities are so unmistakable and so characteristic that the diagnosis is obvious on inspection. This is especially true of the ulnar deviation of the fingers. Other deformities include those of the fingers, flexion deformities of the elbows and knees and valgus deformities of the knees and feet. Subluxation at the metatarsophalangeal joints of the feet leads to the development of painful callosities since the patient is, in effect, walking on his metatarsal heads. This is extremely painful and graphically described as 'walking on marbles'.

However, RA is not just a disease of synovial joints. Tendons and their sheaths are also lined by synovial membrane. Rheumatoid inflammation can involve this lining causing tenosynovitis. Rheumatoid nodules may develop within tendons themselves. Both factors may interfere with the gliding of tendons within their tendon sheaths. The loss of movement, especially in the hands and shoulders, may interfere considerably with normal function. Tendon function may be further embarrassed by their rupture. This may result from erosion of the tendon by aggressive synovium, attrition by a spicule of eroded bone or by weakening from the development of a

nodule within it. This is particularly liable to happen to the
extensor tendons of the hands. Thus not all loss of joint
function is due to joint destruction. Every situation requires
individual analysis.

Extra-articular features

During the course of RA many features appear which involve
non-articular tissues and organs (Fig. 5.3). It is believed that
many of these extra-articular features are due to inflammatory

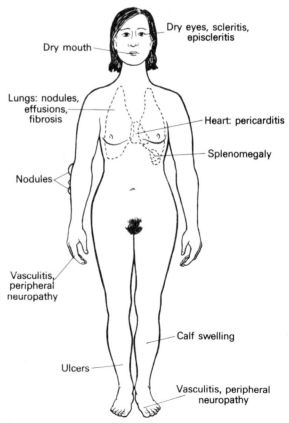

Dry eyes, scleritis,
episcleritis

Dry mouth

Lungs: nodules,
effusions,
fibrosis

Heart: pericarditis

Splenomegaly

Nodules

Vasculitis,
peripheral
neuropathy

Calf swelling

Ulcers

Vasculitis, peripheral
neuropathy

Fig. 5.3. The extra-articular manifestations of rheumatoid arthritis.

changes in small blood vessels. Indeed, this vasculitis is also present in the inflamed synovial membrane itself.

Skin

Generalized sweating is not uncommon and may be a considerable social embarrassment, especially in bed. The skin may be pale from anaemia. With the passage of time the skin

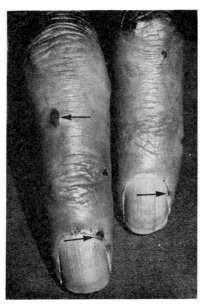

Fig. 5.4. Vasculitic lesions [↗] in the fingers in rheumatoid arthritis. The nail-fold infarcts are characteristic of this condition.

becomes thin and easily liable to damage by simple trauma. This thinning is enhanced by concomitant steroid therapy. Damage to such friable skin, especially round the ankles, may lead to development of ulcers which may become infected. They can be extremely indolent and difficult to heal. However, the classical skin involvement is vasculitis, especially of the fingers, when it is particularly found in the nail folds (Fig. 5.4). Larger blood vessels may also be involved, with the development of ulcers (Fig. 5.5).

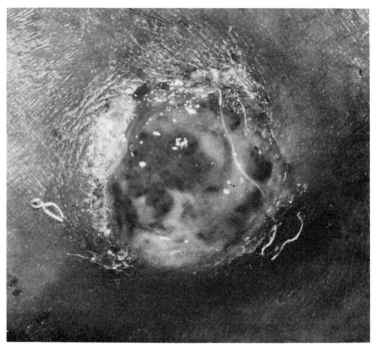

Fig. 5.5. A large, painful and indolent ulcer on the buttock of a rheumatoid patient. Biopsy showed it to be due to vasculitis.

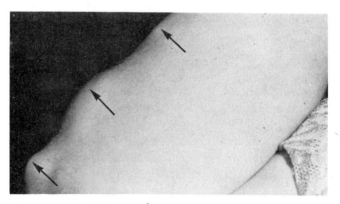

Fig. 5.6. Nodules [↗] at the elbow of a patient with rheumatoid arthritis.

Subcutaneous nodules

Subcutaneous nodules are granulomatous masses found at areas of pressure such as the elbows (Fig. 5.6), the sacrum, the tendo Achillis and other tendons. The overlying skin may break down and infection may be introduced. From this focus septicaemia may develop. Nodules usually recur after surgical excision. They are only occasionally painful. Their presence indicates severe disease. They are an important diagnostic feature in RA and should be carefully looked for.

Lungs

Pleural effusion may occur early in the course of the disease (Fig. 5.7). The fluid is characterized by a very low glucose

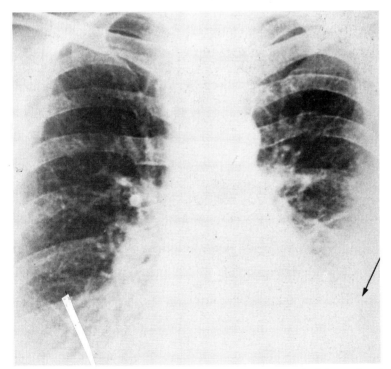

Fig. 5.7. X-ray changes in the lungs in rheumatoid arthritis. On the left is a pleural effusion (↗)

content, the presence of rheumatoid factor and low complement levels. Nevertheless, it should be sent for cytology, to exclude malignant disease, and for bacteriological examination, to exclude infection including tuberculosis. The effusion rarely causes clinical problems although it may occasionally be infected when it presents with the features of empyema. The lung substance itself may develop single or multiple rheumatoid nodules and the distinction from malignant disease may be difficult. Widespread pulmonary fibrosis may develop in severe cases and cause shortness of breath on exertion (Fig. 5.7). This is because the fibrous tissue prevents the diffusion of oxygen from the alveoli into the blood stream. In miners, massive nodule formation and extensive pulmonary fibrosis gives rise to Caplan's syndrome.

Heart

Pericardial effusion may appear. It rarely causes symptoms but can occasionally embarrass cardiac action if it accumulates rapidly (cardiac tamponade). Involvement of the conduction tissue by nodules or inflammatory granulation tissue may cause cardiac arrhythmias.

Eyes

Inflammation of the outer layers of the eye (scleritis and episcleritis) may cause thinning of the sclera and a blue appearance to the eye. Nodules may grow on the sclera. The thinned sclera or a nodule may break down so that the eyeball is perforated. Blindness may ensue if prompt action is not taken. A common complication is dryness of the eyes as part of Sjögren's syndrome. The deficient tear production can be compensated by the installation of artificial tears of methylcellulose into the eye. Iritis and uveitis do not have a particular predisposition for rheumatoid arthritis.

Nervous system

Both the peripheral and central nervous systems may be involved. Compression neuropathies are the commonest neurological manifestations. The median nerve may be compressed in the carpal tunnel, the ulnar nerve at the elbow and cervical nerves by involvement of the neck. Appropriate neurological deficits appear in the hands and arms. Vasculitis of the vasa nervorum supplying blood to peripheral nerves may cause a peripheral neuropathy, especially in the legs, with a 'stocking-type' distribution of sensory disturbance. Occasionally a single nerve may be involved, such as the lateral popliteal, with the production of foot drop. Central nervous system manifestation is usually the result of involvement of the cervical spine. As a result of rheumatoid disease the cervical spine may become subluxated so that there is pressure on the cervical cord. The odontoid peg may press on the cord if the restraining transverse ligament of the atlas has been eroded. Rarely, the odontoid peg may become completely detached from the axis vertebra and migrate upwards through the foramen magnum. Sudden death may be the result. More usually there are signs of an upper motor neurone lesion in the legs with upgoing toes and brisk tendon reflexes. There may be bladder and rectal incontinence and difficulty in walking from the spastic paraplegia. Signs of cord compression in a rheumatoid patient are a neurosurgical emergency. All patients with RA should be carefully examined for cervical spine pathology before any operation and the anaesthetist warned to exercise special caution during intubation. The wearing of a cervical collar by the patient is a potent warning to all the staff in an operating theatre!

Ruptured Baker's cyst

Joint effusions in the knee are common in RA. The fluid may pass posteriorly into the popliteal fossa to form a Baker's cyst. Fluid accumulates here because the opening into the cyst is small and acts as a valve. Fluid enters during movement of the knee, when large intra-articular pressures are generated, but cannot leave it. Although the cyst may be uncomfortable and may prevent full flexion of the knee if it is large and tense, the important complication results from its rupture (Fig. 5.8). Fluid tracks down into the soft tissues of the calf, causing inflammation. Thus the classical signs and symptoms of deep

vein thrombosis are produced: pain in the calf which is
swollen, hot and tender on palpation. This not uncommon
complication is often mistakenly diagnosed as a deep vein
thrombosis and the patient anticoagulated. This treatment is
not only tedious because of the necessity for regular hospital
visits for blood clotting studies but hazardous because of the
danger of haemorrhage. An arthrogram quickly establishes the
diagnosis. Bed rest is the treatment of choice.

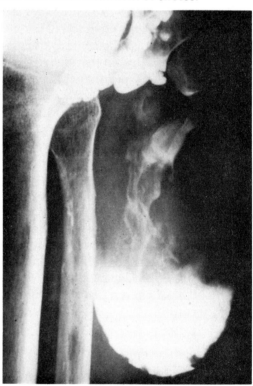

*Fig. 5.8. Contrast medium injected into the knee joint has leaked into the calf of a
patient with rheumatoid arthritis whose popliteal cyst had ruptured.*

Clinical variants of rheumatoid arthritis

There are three clinical variants of RA which need special
mention: Sjögren's syndrome, Felty's syndrome, and juvenile
chronic arthritis.

Sjögren's syndrome

Sjögren's syndrome is characterized clinically by a dry mouth and dry eyes due to decreased production of saliva and tears. Swallowing may be difficult and the eyes may be damaged because of the absence of the cleansing action of tears. The dry mouth cannot be treated but artifical tears are available for the eyes. Sjögren's syndrome can occur in other connective tissue diseases such as systemic lupus erythematosus and scleroderma.

Felty's syndrome

Felty's syndrome is the combination of rheumatoid arthritis with ulcers round about the ankles, splenomegaly and neutropenia. The neutropenia may be severe when the patient is at risk from septicaemia and more localized infections such as in the joints. Infection must be treated with the appropriate antibiotics. The cause of the neutropenia is not clearly understood but splenomegaly may occasionally improve the neutrophil count. The operation has no effect on the course of rheumatoid arthritis which is usually severe and nodular.

Juvenile chronic arthritis

This is an inflammatory polyarthritis occurring in children under the age of 16. It used to be known as Still's disease. It is divided into various types, such as rheumatoid arthritis, the arthritis of systemic lupus erythematosus, ankylosing spondylitis and the arthritis of psoriasis. The management of childhood arthritis poses special problems because the children are still growing. Inflammation around a joint may disturb the bone growth centres and so cause deformities. Furthermore, children must have their educational needs catered for during any prolonged stay in hospital.

Pathology and immunology

Immunological mechanisms

The pathology of RA cannot be understood without knowledge of the immunological mechanisms involved, namely: rheumatoid factors, immune complexes, the complement system, and inflammatory cells.

Rheumatoid factors. Rheumatoid factors are antibodies (immuno-globulins) which can bind onto immunoglobulin G which is normally found in the serum. Thus, in this special case, both the antibody (rheumatoid factors) and the antigen (immuno-globulin G) are immunoglobulins. Rheumatoid factors belong to the M and G class of immunoglobulins. M rheumatoid factors can bind and interact with normal serum immunoglo-bulin G as well as G rheumatoid factors. G rheumatoid factors are rather interesting in that they can interact with each other (thus acting both as antigen and as antibody). Immune complexes are formed as a result of this interaction.

Immune complexes. Immune complexes formed by interaction of rheumatoid factors and the patient's own immunoglobulin G can be found in the serum and joint fluid during the course of the disease. The complexes can be phagocytosed by neutrophils and macrophages, can be deposited in tissues or can activate the complement system. Circulating immune complexes are particularly found in the serum of patients with severe disease, vasculitis and nodules. This is why it is believed that they are involved in the development of these disease manifestations. Since plasma cells, which produce rheumatoid factors, are found in the rheumatoid synovial membrane itself there is active production of immune complexes locally in the joint itself.

The complement system. The complement system is a complex system found in the blood and consisting of a variety of proteins and enzymes. Activation of this system leads to a sequence of events very similar to that occurring in activation of the coagulation cascade and involving many factors. The end result of activation of the complement cascade is the generation of substances with potent inflammatory properties. A convenient way of detecting complement activation is to measure the level of one component, C3. Reduction in its concentration indicates activation. Levels of C3 are indeed decreased in rheumatoid joint fluids, indicating that part of the joint inflammation is due to complement activation. The immune complexes found in RA are particularly good at causing complement activation.

Inflammatory cells. The deposition of immune complexes themselves and the activation of the complement system lead to the release of materials which powerfully attract inflammatory cells to these tissue sites. The inflammatory cells consist of neutrophils, macrophages and lymphocytes. The first two are phagocytic. They ingest immune complexes and, during this process, release enzymes which digest ligaments, tendons, cartilage and bone. The lymphocytes are chronic inflammatory cells which maintain the inflammation both by their own efforts and by stimulating the macrophages.

Pathology

The deposition of immune complexes and complement activation lead to the development of vasculitis. This is the pathological basis for many of the extra-articular features of the disease. However, vasculitis is also found in the synovial membrane. The signs of joint inflammation, which are such important clinical features of the disease, are the outcome of these two mechanisms.

Nevertheless, deposition of immune complexes and complement activation cannot be the whole story since they also occur in other diseases such as lupus erythematosus in which joint destruction does not take place. The main difference lies in the histology of the synovial membrane. The synovial membrane in RA is hypertrophied and highly vascular, and is packed with inflammatory cells such as lymphocytes and macrophages. It is an aggressive tissue growing into bone and cartilage, and

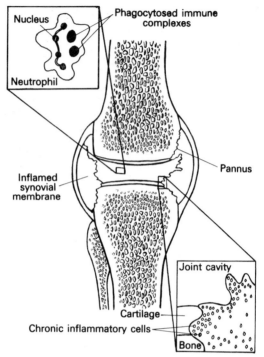

Fig. 5.9. Diagram showing pannus invading articular cartilage and bone to cause erosions, and cells in the joint fluid which have phagocytosed immune complexes.

destroying them to produce the characteristic erosions and loss of joint space seen on X-rays. This inflamed, aggressive, eroding tissue is known as the pannus (Fig. 5.9).

Diagnosis

The diagnosis of RA is made primarily on clinical grounds since there is no specific test. Nevertheless, some help may be provided by laboratory investigations.

Blood

There is usually a moderate hypochromic, normocytic anaemia. If there has been gastrointestinal bleeding because of

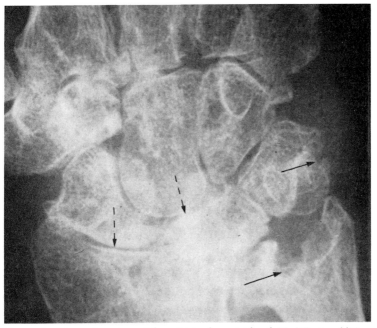

Fig. 5.10. Advanced erosions of the wrist in rheumatoid arthritis (↗). In addition, there is joint narrowing (↗) and osteoporosis.

the drugs being taken then the anaemia may be the iron-deficient type with a hypochromic, microcytic picture. The erythrocyte sedimentation rate is elevated. In the serum the concentration of immunoglobulins is increased. M rheumatoid factor, detected by agglutination tests, is elevated.

Radiology

Radiological changes in the early stages of the disease may reveal nothing more than juxta-articular osteoporosis. Later, the more usual changes of loss of joint space (due to destruction of cartilage) and erosion of bone are seen (Fig. 5.10). In the more chronic stage the radiological changes of secondary osteoarthrosis may supervene (see Chapter 3). Extra-articular manifestations involving the heart and lungs may be seen on chest X-rays.

Synovial fluid

The synovial fluid has a low viscosity and high cell count, and contains rheumatoid factor. The C3 level is decreased. Fluid should always be sent for microbiological examination as rheumatoid joints are liable to superadded bacterial infection.

Synovial membrane

Open or closed biopsy of the joint may allow histological examination of the membrane. This will show the inflammatory changes already described under Pathology.

Management

Since the etiology of RA is unknown there is no specific therapy. The patient is managed with continuous supervision by a team consisting of physician, nurse, physiotherapist, occupational therapist and orthopaedic surgeon. Today the conventional stereotype of the rheumatoid patient as a deformed individual confined to wheelchair or bed and completely dependent on others is fortunately becoming less common, although such unfortunate cases still occur. Even in such individuals this stage should not be reached until many years of disease activity have passed. Constant attention to detail is important. Thus an excessively inflamed joint should alert one to the possibility of infection. Sudden loss of function may indicate tendon involvement. If tenosynovitis is the cause then steroid injections may terminate this inflammatory episode. Tendon rupture may be amenable to surgical repair. Intra-articular steroid injections have kept many patients independent and at work. They should be used as often as is necessary despite the theoretical risk of accelerated destruction of the articular cartilage.

6

Seronegative Arthritis

G. S. Panayi

Seronegative arthritis differs from rheumatoid arthritis in the following important respects:

1. Rheumatoid factor absent
2. Asymmetrical joint inflammation
3. Male preponderance
4. Involvement of sacroiliac joints and spine
5. Iritis
6. Heredity

Some of these differences are not always absolute. Thus in some types the peripheral joint inflammation may be symmetrical. The main diseases in this group are:

1. Ankylosing spondylitis
2. Psoriatic arthritis
3. Arthritis of inflammatory bowel disease
4. Reiter's syndrome
5. Reactive arthritis

The prototype disease is ankylosing spondylitis. Like rheumatoid arthritis, their cause is not known although infection is thought to be the most likely possibility. In some of them, the infectious agent is actually known. One common link between all these diseases is involvement of the sacroiliac joints and the spine. Hence an alternative name is the 'pelvospondylitides'.

Heredity in seronegative arthritis

The discovery of a hereditary aspect in seronegative arthritis
has been one of the most exciting recent developments in
medicine. Everyone is familiar with the concept of blood
groups. These are antigens present on the surface of red blood
cells. They are hereditary factors and are the products of genes
received from the parents.

When organs, such as the kidney, began to be grafted it was
soon realized that here also there ought to be compatibility
between the donor and the recipient if the transplant was not to
be rejected by the recipient. It was found that a completely

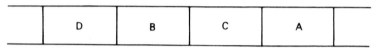

Fig. 6.1. Arrangement of the four known HLA genes on the human sixth chromosome.

different group of antigens was responsible for graft incom-
patibility. They were found on all nucleated cells. For
convenience, lymphocytes, which can be obtained easily and in
large numbers from the peripheral blood, were used to tissue-
type individuals involved in organ transplantation. Hence
these antigens were called 'human leucocyte antigens' or HLA
in short. These antigens are the products on the cell surface of
genes received from the parents. By ingenious experiments it
was found that these genes are present on the human sixth
chromosome. By family studies the order in which these genes
are arranged on the chromosome was determined (Fig. 6.1).
The genes have been given letters to distinguish one from the
other and the different antigens determined by each gene given
a number. Thus in tissue-typing one may detect antigens such
as A1, B8, C5 and so on. The apparently illogical arrangement
of these genes on chromosome six is merely the result of the
order in which they were discovered.

These tissue-typing antigens are found in all mammals.
Experiments soon showed that the ability of an animal to
mount a good immune response was determined by whether it
had a particular antigen. Since it is known that many human

Table 6.1. HLA and disease associations

Disease	HLA antigen	Percentage of patients having the antigen
Ankylosing spondylitis	B27	90
Iritis	B27	30
Psoriatic arthritis	B38	80
Multiple sclerosis	D2	70
Rheumatoid arthritis	D4	75

diseases, not least the rheumatic diseases, have immunological aspects, the role of HLA antigens was investigated. Some very interesting associations were found and these are shown in Table 6.1. The possession of one of these antigens increases the risk of developing the particular disease associated with it. Thus being born with the antigen HLA-B27 increases the risk of ankylosing spondylitis some 300 times, and HLA-D4 increases the risk of rheumatoid arthritis some 10 times. It is still not known why having one of these antigens increases the chance of developing disease. It may be that the individual is more likely to react immunologically to an environmental agent, such as bacteria or viruses, with the development of the disease.

Ankylosing spondylitis

Epidemiology

Ankylosing spondylitis occurs in about one per thousand of the population. It is much commoner in males. However, with the recent recognition that HLA-B27 positive individuals are more susceptible to the disease, it is thought to be more common than this and to have a more equal sex incidence. This is probably because many people, and especially women, are likely to dismiss back pain as just 'one of those things' with which one has to live. It can occur at any age, even in childhood when it is one form of juvenile chronic arthritis. The other seronegative arthritides may also occur in childhood.

Nevertheless, the commonest age of onset is in the late teens or early twenties.

Clinical features

The main features of the disease are pelvospondylitis, peripheral arthritis and iritis. The sites affected are shown in Fig. 6.2. The pelvospondylitis manifests itself as pain and stiffness in the low back, especially in the early hours of the morning. Exercise alleviates the symptoms. The thoracic and cervical spines can also be involved with similar symptoms in

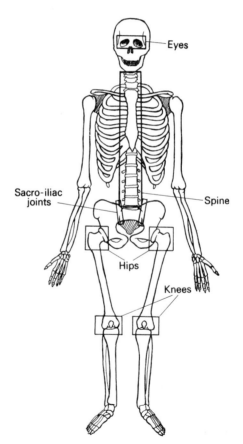

Fig. 6.2. The main sites affected in akylosing spondylitis.

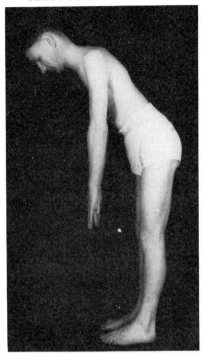

Fig. 6.3. Abnormal posture in ankylosing spondylitis. The patient is attempting to flex his spine. Note the poor range of movement, and the straight and rigid lumbar region of the spine.

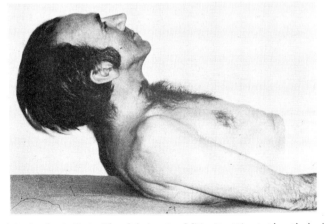

Fig. 6.4. Another patient with ankylosing spondylitis attempting to place the back of his head onto the couch. He is unable to do so because of bony fusion of the cervical vertebrae and joints.

the relevant areas. The peripheral arthritis involves especially
the larger joints such as the hips, knees and elbows. Like all
inflamed joints they are particularly stiff and painful in the
mornings on waking. The iritis causes a red, painful eye with
diminution in visual acuity. Since this is a serious compli
cation, which may cause blindness, all patients should be
routinely asked about eye symptoms.

The disease may relapse and remit. With the passage of time
the back becomes increasingly stiff and immobile. Exami
nation reveals loss of all lumbar spinal movements, the loss
depending on the duration of the disease and its severity, poor
or non-existent chest expansion and reduced movements of the
cervical spine. The spine displays a characteristic series of
deformities with the loss of the normal lumbar lordosis,
development of dorsal kyphosis and the neck held in a forward
flexed position (Figs 6.3 and 6.4). The involved peripheral
joints, especially the hips, may be destroyed by the inflam
matory process so that they are painful and have reduced
movement.

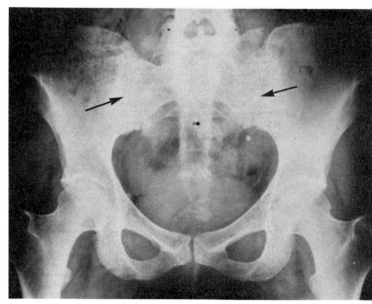

*Fig. 6.5. Radiological changes in ankylosing spondylitis. There is almost complete
obliteration of the sacro-iliac joints (↗) with sclerosis of the bone on either side.*

Investigation

During the active, inflammatory stage of the disease the erythrocyte sedimentation rate is elevated. Rheumatoid factor is absent from both the serum and any joint fluid aspirated. Joint fluid analysis shows an inflammatory picture with absence of crystals. Radiological examination provides the best diagnosis. The sacroiliac joints show erosive changes in the early stages, and complete bony fusion in the late stages (Fig. 6.5). Newer techniques employing joint scanning with radioactive technetium show increased uptake of the isotope during the active stage before X-rays reveal any abnormalities. In the

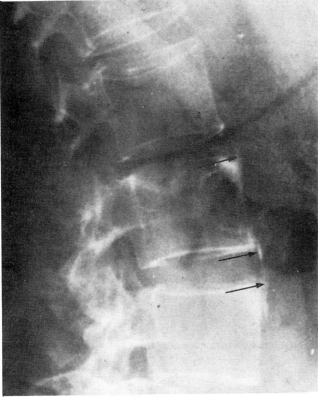

Fig. 6.6. Lateral radiograph of the lumbar spine in moderately early ankylosing spondylitis. Bony outgrowths (syndesmophytes) are beginning to unite the vertebral bodies (↗).

spine the earliest change is 'squaring' of the vertebral bodies
(Fig. 6.6). Later there is bony fusion between the vertebrae and
across the intervertebral discs, and ossification of the ligaments
of the spine and of the apophyseal joints. This gives rise to the
classical appearance of the 'bamboo spine'. In the joints there
is loss of joint space due to destruction of the articular
cartilage.

Pathology

The pathology of the disease is not clearly understood as few
patients ever come to autopsy. It is believed that immune
complexes play no part in the disease. This is completely unlike
the situation in rheumatoid arthritis, and explains why extra-
articular manifestations such as nodules, vasculitis and lung
fibrosis do not occur in ankylosing spondylitis. The earliest
change is invasion of involved areas of the spine by chronic
inflammatory cells, which cause localized tissue damage and
activate new bone formation. Why this should be so is also not
known. Eventually the new bone buries the inflammation.
Clinically this can be detected by the presence of a completely
immobile but pain-free back. Bony ankylosis or periarticular
new bone formation may also take place in the hip joint.

Management

Pain and inflammation are managed with the appropriate
drugs (see Chapter 11). Physiotherapy is one of the most
valuable aspects of the management of ankylosing spondylitis.
Its aims are to maintain the maximum range of back
movements and to teach the patient correct posture. Correct
posture includes sleeping on a firm, non-sagging mattress with
one small or, preferably, no pillow. Since the back will
eventually fuse into an immobile, rigid column, correct
posture will at least allow this fusion to occur in the best
possible functional position. For example, fusion of the
cervical spine in a flexed position may impede forward vision
which is a tremendous incapacity. Despite the rigidity and poor
expansion of the thoracic cage, due to fusion of the ribs to the

dorsal spine, chest infections are rarely a serious problem. Hip involvement is more serious. Total hip arthroplasty may be necessary. Other forms of orthopaedic surgery should hardly ever be necessary.

Psoriatic arthritis

Psoriatic arthritis occurs in about one per thousand of the population but in up to 10 per cent of patients with psoriasis. It is characterized by inflammation of the sacroiliac joints and the spine as well as of the peripheral joints. The former resembles the pelvospondylitis of ankylosing spondylitis and is similarly associated with HLA-B27 antigen. The peripheral arthritis may involve many joints or a few of the larger ones. Like rheumatoid arthritis, it may be destructive with erosion of the articular cartilage and bone. Indeed, in some patients the destruction may be so severe that this aggressive form of the disease has been called 'arthritis mutilans'. A characteristic finding, not present in rheumatoid arthritis, is the involvement of the distal interphalangeal joints with swelling, heat, tenderness on palpation and pain.

Investigation and management are as for ankylosing spondylitis. Two points should be remembered about psoriatic arthritis. First, the evidence for psoriasis may be very scanty and consist simply of pitting of the nails or an extremely small skin lesion hidden in the umbilicus, the natal cleft or in the scalp. On occasion the arthritis may precede the psoriasis by many years. Second, the increased turnover of cells in the areas of skin involved by psoriasis may lead to an elevation in the plasma concentration of uric acid. Sometimes this hyperuricaemia or associated gouty arthritis may need appropriate treatment.

Arthritis of inflammatory bowel disease

Crohn's disease and ulcerative colitis are inflammatory diseases involving predominantly the small and large intestines respectively. They are relatively rare, occurring in two of every one hundred thousand of the population. Their interest lies in that they may occasionally be associated with an arthritis. This occurs in 3 to 10 per cent of patients and may be peripheral inflammatory arthritis, pelvospondylitis, or both. The arthritic manifestations are similar to those of ankylosing spondylitis. Like the latter, iritis may occur and the pelvospondylitis is often HLA-B27 positive.

Reiter's syndrome

Reiter's syndrome affects young men. Its features are conjunctivitis, urethritis or a dysenteric illness and arthritis. It may be short-lived or chronic. It may cause little or no joint destruction but on occasions the joint damage, particularly in the lower limbs, may be severe and disabling. It shares many features with the seronegative arthritides already described. Those patients who are HLA-B27 positive may develop pelvospondylitis. A characteristic skin eruption can occur and it is almost identical histologically with psoriasis. Heel pain, with the formation of a calcaneal spur, is another common feature.

Reactive arthritis

It has long been known that some persons after intestinal infection with known microorganisms (such as *Yersinia enterocolitica, Salmonella* or *Shigella*) can develop an inflammatory arthritis. The reason for this association was unknown until it was found that most of those who developed the arthritis were also HLA-B27 positive. Because of distinctive association between the known intestinal infection, the arthritis and the tissue antigen, this syndrome is called 'reactive arthritis'. It forms an interesting link between ankylosing spondylitis and Reiter's syndrome. The existence of reactive arthritis lends hope to the belief that ankylosing spondylitis may itself be related to infection. Clinically, reactive arthritis is usually a self-limiting condition.

7

Connective Tissue Diseases

T. J. Gibson

It is conventional to categorize the following well-defined disease states under the heading of connective tissue diseases:

Rheumatoid disease
Systemic lupus erythematosus (SLE)
Scleroderma (progressive systemic sclerosis or PSS)
Polyarteritis nodosa (PAN)
Dermatomyositis
Polymyositis
Mixed connective tissue disease (MCTD)
Polymyalgia rheumatica

As many of these disease states share certain clinical and laboratory features, it is justifiable to consider them together. However, their disease patterns, histopathology and probably causes are distinct. Sometimes they are referred to as the collagen or collagen-vascular diseases but neither of these terms is any more appropriate than 'connective tissue disease' since none of them convey any real insight into the basic disorder. With the exception of rheumatoid arthritis (see Chapter 5) and polymyalgia, most are relatively uncommon diseases in the United Kingdom.

Systemic lupus erythematosus (SLE)

Systemic lupus erythematosus has attracted more attention than its prevalence would suggest. It is associated with the

formation of antibodies directed against human cell components and these antibodies may be important aspects of the
disease pathology. It has been extensively studied as the prime
model of a disease associated with, and possibly caused by,
immune phenomena. Occasionally, the disease is associated
with the consumption of specific drugs and remits when these
are discontinued.

SLE is much more common amongst females than males
and is especially prevalent in North America where it exhibits a
predilection for the black population. The reasons for this
distribution are unknown.

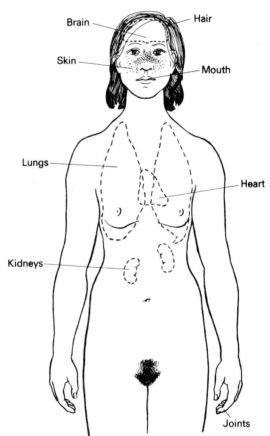

Fig. 7.1. Distribution of areas which may be involved in SLE.

Symptoms and signs

The most common features are joint pain, skin rashes, photo-sensitivity, alopecia, Raynaud's phenomenon, pleurisy, pericarditis, convulsions, psychiatric disturbance, renal disease and mouth ulcers. Fig. 7.1 shows the areas of the body which may be involved.

Most often the clinical picture unfolds over a period of months or years. Manifestations may occur consecutively and appear as a series of separate episodes of ill-health or, less often, many features may appear simultaneously. Diagnosis can be considerably aided by characteristic laboratory findings.

The arthropathy may take the form of peripheral joint pain and stiffness, with or without evidence of joint inflammation. When present, the features of arthritis may be similar to those of early rheumatoid disease with swelling, tenderness and warmth, particularly of the small joints of the fingers. The arthritis is frequently periodic. Joint deformities and subsequent dysfunction are rare and when they arise they are more likely caused by tendon involvement. X-rays reveal none of the articular erosion and destruction associated with rheumatoid arthritis.

Skin involvement may take several forms. The classical pattern is the so-called butterfly rash across the face. This is much less common than non-specific rashes such as hives, bullous blisters or simple erythema. Exposure to sunlight may provoke a rash on exposed areas or may actually activate disease involvement at other sites. A small proportion of patients with discoid lupus erythematosus, a disease usually confined to skin, may develop features of SLE. Evolution from cutaneous to systemic disease in these patients may extend over several years or decades. Patchy alopecia may coincide with overall disease activity and may be transient or recurrent (Fig. 7.2).

Raynaud's phenomenon is common in all the connective tissue diseases. It is one of the less specific manifestations of SLE.

Episodes of chest pain can usually be ascribed to either pleurisy or pericarditis. Small patches of pneumonia may be

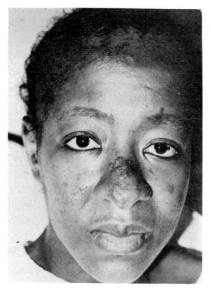

Fig. 7.2. A girl with SLE showing alopecia and the rash of discoid lupus.

detected radiologically, often in the absence of chest symptoms. Respiratory function studies suggest that the lungs are involved more frequently than symptoms and X-rays would suggest.

Nervous system involvement and kidney disease each afflict more than half of the patients with SLE. The most common neurological features are grand mal convulsions, headaches and psychiatric disturbance, such as changes of mood or psychotic behaviour. Many other patterns of nervous system disease have been documented reflecting the potential involvement of any area of the brain, spinal cord or peripheral nerves.

Kidney involvement may be detected by the presence of blood or protein in the urine. The latter may be excreted in sufficient quantity to cause the nephrotic syndrome. Under the microscope, the presence of red blood cells and renal casts provides further evidence of active kidney disease. Three distinct patterns of renal glomerulonephritis are recognizable on light microscopy (Fig. 7.3). A diffuse increase of the glomerular capillary cells—diffuse proliferative pattern—usually denotes that the patient will develop progressive

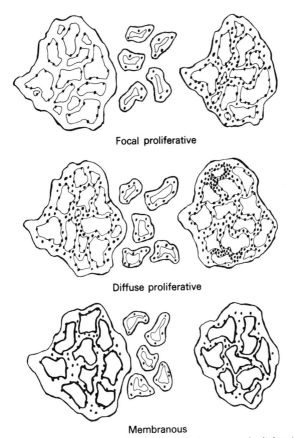

Focal proliferative

Diffuse proliferative

Membranous

Fig. 7.3. The three main patterns of renal histopathology seen under light microscopy.

renal impairment. The two other patterns—membranous and focal proliferative—imply a better outlook but exceptions arise and the histological patterns are not mutually exclusive. Renal disease remains the most feared complication of SLE; research into effective treatments of lupus has been largely directed toward management of the glomerulonephritis.

Laboratory features

The hallmark of SLE is the demonstration of antibodies in the blood directed against constituents of the cell nucleus (antinuclear antibody or factor: ANA or ANF). Presence of one of these antibodies was previously confirmed by the detection of LE cells which are found when blood from a patient with SLE is incubated. Cell nuclei damaged by antibodies directed against them become swollen, disgorged by their cells and engulfed by polymorph white cells to form the LE cells. This test has been superseded although it is still performed by many laboratories. ANF is now more commonly detected by an indirect method using immunofluorescent staining of animal cells incubated with patients' serum. This test demonstrates the presence of antibodies against deoxyribonucleic acid (DNA) as well as antibodies against several other constituents of the cell nucleus. Antibodies against pure DNA are more specific for SLE and are detectable by the techniques of DNA binding and the *Crithidia luciliae* tests. When positive, these investigations are of great diagnostic value. A disadvantage of the ANF test is its lack of specificity and although it is the standard laboratory method of screening for SLE, a positive result may be seen in other diseases such as rheumatoid arthritis or scleroderma. Measurement of serum complement is commonly performed. When the level is low it may be presumed that serum complement is being rapidly utilized by antibody–antigen reactions. This may provide confirmatory evidence of SLE activity, particularly of renal involvement but is not by itself a reliable indicator of progressive disease.

A range of haematological or serological abnormalities may occur. Mild anaemia and a raised ESR are usual but not specific. Haemolytic anaemia with a positive Coomb's test is sufficiently common to be considered a diagnostic criterion, as are reduced white blood cells and platelets. Sometimes standard tests for syphilis are positive but the more specific tests for treponemal infection are negative. A biological false positive test for syphilis may also be a helpful diagnostic finding.

Other laboratory findings may include proteins which precipitate when serum is stored in the cold (cryoglobulins) and less commonly, antibodies which impair blood coagulation.

Treatment

Management of this disorder is difficult and even controversial. Recognition that the majority of patients have a good long-term prognosis has made many doctors more circumspect in their use of available treatments, some of which are potentially harmful. In the last 20 years, there has been a measurable improvement in the outlook of patients with SLE. This may be ascribed to the recognition of milder forms of the illness and a more conservative approach to drug therapy rather than any radical innovations of treatment.

Many patients with this illness are unnecessarily anxious because they may have learned of its more severe manifestations. When their questions are answered in terms of probability patients can be greatly reassured. General advice should include a caution against prolonged exposure to direct sunlight since even those with no suggestive previous history may experience worsening of their illness in this situation. Sunscreen lotions probably lessen the risks.

Many sufferers are young women and whether pregnancy should be contemplated is a question frequently raised. Assuming a patient is not rapidly deteriorating or very ill, pregnancy need not be discouraged and normal deliveries of healthy infants can be anticipated. However, the chances of miscarriage are increased and occasionally the disease is activated by pregnancy.

The major drug used in treatment is the corticosteroid, prednisolone. Corticosteroids have many harmful effects and prolonged use of high doses may cause morbidity worse than the disease itself. Infection is a relatively common cause of death and the risks of serious infection are greatly increased by prednisolone. As a general principle, patients are given just sufficient to control disease activity. Ideally, patients should be controlled without recourse to steroids and it is possible to treat many with only aspirin or similar drugs.

Renal involvement constitutes the most difficult area of treatment. There is some evidence that aggressive treatment of patients with the more severe histopathological pattern of kidney involvement improves the outlook. There is no general agreement as to the best approach and treatments now in use include large doses of prednisolone (sometimes given intravenously), immunosuppressive agents (such as azathioprine) and anticoagulants. There are advocates for each of these drug therapies or their combinations. Their relative efficacy is controversial and, in particular, the usefulness of immunosuppressives is disputed.

Other treatments are currently being investigated but none has so far been shown to exert a predictably beneficial effect. One of these, the removal and separation of patients' plasma containing potentially harmful proteins (immune complexes) and the transfusion of fresh plasma is known as plasmapheresis and seems promising.

Severe involvement of the nervous system may constitute another life-threatening manifestation but unlike renal disease there has been little research into how this can be best managed. Large doses of steroids have been recommended but there is some evidence that this approach may actually worsen the prognosis.

In general the drug treatment of SLE is arbitrary and since the disease is so frequently episodic, therapy has to be modulated. Despite the uncertainties associated with treatment the prognosis for most patients with SLE is good.

Scleroderma (progressive systemic sclerosis)

Like SLE scleroderma occurs more frequently in females. It shares some of the laboratory features of SLE but can usually be readily distinguished from this and other connective tissue diseases. Fig. 7.4 shows the main sites which may be affected.

Symptoms and signs

There is a wide spectrum of disease severity. The most common manifestation is Raynaud's phenomenon and this may precede other features by years. Skin involvement is the most characteristic clinical aspect of the disease. Initially this may appear as

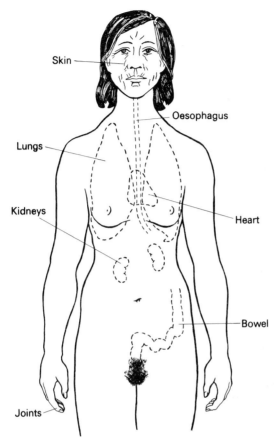

Fig. 7.4. *The main sites which may be affected in progressive systemic sclerosis.*

diffuse swelling over the hands, feet or other sites. With time, the skin becomes taut and apparently bound to underlying tissues. This process may involve the face (causing loss of normal forehead wrinkling and a reduced oral aperture (Fig. 7.5), the trunk, limbs and digits (causing impaired joint movement or flexion deformities) (Fig. 7.6). Telangiectasia over the face, lips and trunk are commonly found in conjunction with these changes. Calcification (calcinosis) may occur in the skin and particularly over the fingers where it may extrude through painful ulcers. The tips of the fingers may appear

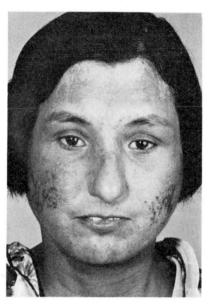

Fig. 7.5. Facial involvement in progressive systemic sclerosis. There is tightening of the skin with loss of normal skin lines and narrowing of the mouth aperture.

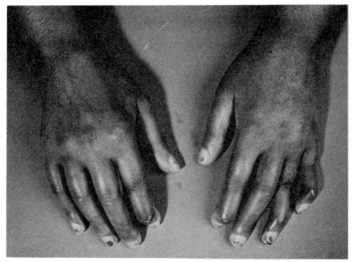

Fig. 7.6. Hands of a patient with progressive systemic sclerosis showing tightening of the skin and finger contractures.

tapered or stunted and X-rays of the digits may show associated resorption of the distal bone. The concurrence of calcinosis, Raynaud's phenomenon, sclerodactyly and telangiectasia is sometimes referred to as the CRST syndrome. Older reports notwithstanding, this constellation of symptoms confers no special benefits and represents but one phase of this often progressive disease.

Localized scleroderma (morphoea) is usually discussed in the context of generalized scleroderma. This comprises a well-defined skin lesion usually on the face or trunk, sometimes forming a broad linear band or associated with atrophy of underlying tissues. Occasionally this may be confused with the cutaneous changes of scleroderma.

The joints in scleroderma are not affected to any great extent but joint pain and stiffness may occur. Synovial swelling and effusions tend to be slight. Cartilage loss is not demonstrable on X-ray although rare instances of joint erosion, similar to that of rheumatoid arthritis, have been recorded. Tendon sheath inflammation and restricted tendon movement together with skin tautening contribute largely to joint deformities.

Although the visible manifestations of the disease may be serious, involvement of other organs has more sinister implications. Unlike SLE scleroderma tends to be relentlessly progressive rather than intermittently active. Deterioration may be insidious. Development of symptoms suggesting systemic involvement usually denotes advanced disease. Dysphagia or indigestion are likely to imply oesophageal involvement with loss of peristalsis and dilatation. Diarrhoea usually reflects loss of small bowel motility and this aspect of the disease occasionally results in malabsorption.

The increased fibrosis which affects the skin may also occur in the lungs; pulmonary fibrosis may be sufficiently severe to produce dyspnoea and respiratory failure. Involvement of the heart may be reflected by pericarditis, abnormal heart rhythms and heart failure. The kidneys may also be affected. A large proportion of patients develop a mild glomerulonephritis. A smaller percentage are afflicted by a rapid deterioration of renal function associated with marked hypertension.

Investigation

As with the other connective tissue diseases, anaemia and marked elevation of the ESR are common. Some of the laboratory features found in SLE may also be shared by scleroderma.although with less consistency. The test for ANF may be positive although the specific tests for antibodies

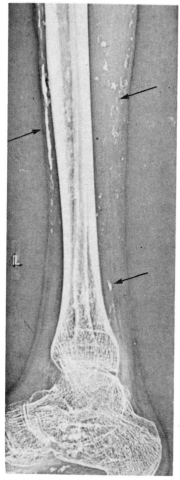

Fig. 7.7. Xeroradiograph showing subcutaneous calcification in progressive systemic sclerosis (↗).

against pure (native) DNA tend to be normal. Biological false tests for syphilis and the Coomb's test may be positive. Renal involvement may be first manifested by finding proteinuria or haematuria.

X-rays may reveal areas of subcutaneous calcification (Fig. 7.7) and loss of bone at the tip of the digits. Views of the chest frequently indicate some degree of pulmonary fibrosis. Barium studies of the gastrointestinal tract will confirm involvement of the oesophagus or small bowel. Special manometric studies which can detect disorders of motility may determine disease at these sites long before symptoms are apparent and before barium X-rays become abnormal.

Treatment

Although the disease is invariably progressive the prognosis varies widely. Those with rapid renal failure and hypertension fare worst and early involvement of heart or lungs is associated with a worse outlook.

Management is entirely symptomatic. Pain may be alleviated by analgesics. Corticosteroids have no effect on disease progression and their use is confined to limiting acute, distressing manifestations such as pericarditis. Much attention has been focused on the use of D-penicillamine but there is little evidence that this drug does more than improve skin involvement in a few patients.

Physiotherapy and appropriate use of splintage may be remarkably effective in correcting flexion deformities and improving the range of joint movement.

Mixed connective tissue disease (MCTD)

It has recently become appreciated that a small group of patients have overlapping features of SLE, scleroderma and even rheumatoid arthritis. Such patients may exhibit arthritis, Raynaud's phenomenon, characteristic 'sausage-shaped' digits, rashes, pleurisy, pericarditis and laboratory features suggesting SLE. This group may be positively identified by demon-

stration of high concentrations of serum antibodies to ribo-
nucleoprotein (RNP). The same antibody may also be found in
patients with SLE and scleroderma although in much smaller
quantities. Initially it was thought that patients in this category
of so-called mixed connective tissue disease were spared renal
involvement and enjoyed a good prognosis. Subsequently it
has become apparent that renal disease does occur, as may
other severe manifestations. Some doctors have questioned
whether the demonstration of high levels of RNP antibody
carries any special significance. Others doubt whether mixed
connective tissue disease should be considered as an entity.

Dermatomyositis and polymyositis

Inflammation of muscle causes weakness and wasting of the
areas where muscle bulk is most evident: the limb girdles.
Myositis may be a feature of both SLE and scleroderma. This
association, together with occasional joint pain, stiffness,
Raynaud's phenomenon and pulmonary fibrosis make it
reasonable to consider dermatomyositis and polymyositis with
the connective tissue diseases.

Symptoms and signs

Weakness is usually the major complaint. The onset may be
abrupt and the patient may experience difficulty in raising the
arms or climbing stairs. Weakness of the pharyngeal muscles
results in a nasal voice and dysphagia. Loss of muscle power is
easily demonstrable and inability to raise the head from the
pillow against mild resistance is typical. Muscles may be slightly
tender. Wasting follows in the course of time.

An accompanying erythematous rash over the extensor
creases of the fingers, the knees, groins or face would suggest
skin and muscle involvement: dermatomyositis. The rash may
be particularly evident beneath the eyes and may be associated
with facial puffiness.

Investigation

Except when associated with other connective tissue diseases, the laboratory hallmarks of these conditions, e.g. ANF test, are absent. Diagnosis is established by confirming the presence of muscle skin disease by electromyography, muscle damage by demonstrating raised serum enzymes such as creatine phosphokinase (CPK) and muscle inflammation by examining biopsy tissue for inflammation and muscle fibre necrosis.

In middle-aged or elderly patients there is a strong link between dermatomyositis and malignant disease. The association with polymyositis is less clear but in either case, the diagnosis is incomplete until a search for a hidden tumour has been carried out.

Treatment

Modest doses of corticosteroids are worth attempting. Some patients will improve dramatically. Response can be monitored by serial estimations of serum enzymes. Unfortunately steroids do not always induce a clear improvement and their long-term use in large doses is to be deprecated because of the risks entailed (see p. 103). Immunosuppressive agents such as methotrexate, either alone or in conjunction with steroids, may succeed where steroids alone have failed. The disease may remit spontaneously. The effect of eradicating malignancy when it co-exists is unpredictable.

Weakness and debility make some patients totally dependent on nursing care while the disease is at its most severe. Weak chest wall muscles, the risk of inhalation and concomitant steroid treatment result in a high incidence of chest infection. Tube feeding may be necessary to prevent inhalation pneumonia. Regular chest physiotherapy and pharyngeal suction may be vital in lessening this risk. During the period of recovery strengthening exercises aid the patient's return to independence.

Polyarteritis nodosa

Inflammation of blood vessels may be a feature of SLE, rheumatoid arthritis and scleroderma. Vasculitis may also occur in several other disease states such as Henoch-Schönlein purpura and temporal arteritis but all of these can be distinguished from polyarteritis on a clinical basis. Polyarteritis affects men more than women. A proportion of cases arise in association with the presence of circulating hepatitis B antigen (Australia antigen).

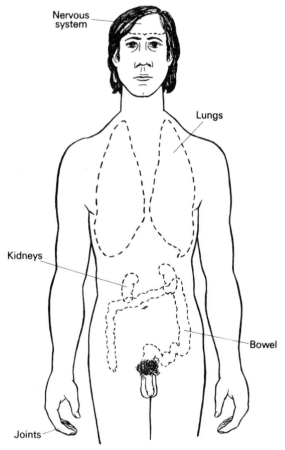

Fig. 7.8. The sites and organs which may be affected in polyarteritis nodosa.

Widespread arterial involvement may result in vessel occlusion, small aneurysms and haemorrhage. The disease usually carries an extremely poor prognosis but is fortunately rare.

Symptoms and signs

The distribution of clinical features reflects that of the arteritis. Fig. 7.8 shows the sites which may be affected. Abdominal pain with blood-stained diarrhoea, peripheral neuropathy and central nervous system signs including stroke, are multisystem features which should suggest the diagnosis. Joint pain may be present but a florid arthritis does not occur. Renal involvement is common with progressive renal dysfunction and hyper-

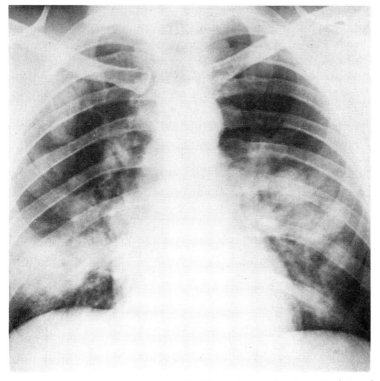

Fig. 7.9. Chest X-ray of a patient with Wegener's granulomatosis. Widespread granulomata have involved both lungs.

tension. When the lungs are affected the patient may exhibit a picture of small airways obstruction. Dyspnoea and cough may be associated with X-ray evidence of patchy consolidation. Fever is a usual but unhelpful diagnostic feature. The association of sinusitis and obvious pulmonary involvement would suggest a diagnosis of Wegener's granulomatosis, a condition closely allied to that of polyarteritis nodosa.

Diagnosis is very difficult to establish with certainty. Examination of involved organ tissue under the microscope offers the most reasonable prospect. However, the risk of bleeding following blind attempts at biopsy of organs like the kidney may deter investigation. Arteriography of specified areas of disease, e.g. the brain or mesenteric vessels, may demonstrate small aneurysms which are thought to be diagnostic.

When bronchial obstruction is present an increase of blood eosinophils may be seen. Chest X-ray may reveal multiple opacities in the lung fields. Such changes are considered characteristic of Wegener's granulomatosis when they are rounded or cavitated (Fig. 7.9). However, the distinction may be more a question of semantics since polyarteritis nodosa and Wegener's are probably variants of the same pathological process.

Treatment

The response of polyarteritis nodosa to treatment tends to be disappointing. Corticosteroids occasionally induce remission. The use of immunosuppressive drugs such as cyclophosphamide may be associated with a better outcome and there is ample evidence that this form of treatment will improve the prognosis of those with Wegener's granulomatosis. For most patients, polyarteritis nodosa proves eventually to be a fatal illness.

Polymyalgia rheumatica and temporal arteritis

Polymyalgia rheumatica is much more prevalent in the United Kingdom than any of the connective tissue diseases so far discussed. Most doctors now agree that there is a link between polymyalgia and temporal arteritis. The majority believe that they are the same disease. Almost invariably the disease affects the elderly segment of the population. It is rare in patients less than 50 years of age. Women are affected more than men.

Symptoms and signs

Polymyalgia usually begins abruptly. The cardinal symptoms are proximal muscle pain and stiffness. The patient may suddenly find difficulty with simple tasks such as dressing. A striking absence of clinical signs is characteristic. Temporal arteritis (cranial or giant cell arteritis) may be clinically demonstrable in patients whose symptoms are confined to muscle. Tenderness and thickening of the temporal arteries or tenderness of the scalp at other sites should be sought. In classical temporal arteritis, the main complaint is headache. Facial pain on chewing is occasionally seen. The scalp symptoms may be preceded by, or associated with, the muscle symptoms of polymyalgia. The major hazard of temporal arteritis is the involvement of branches of the ophthalmic artery which may cause catastrophic and irreversible blindness. This complication demands that temporal arteritis–polymyalgia be treated promptly. Rarely, large vessels may be involved by the arteritis, giving rise to occlusion of blood flow to parts of the brain or other vital organs.

Investigation

The combination of muscle pain, stiffness and a very high ESR in an elderly patient denotes polymyalgia rheumatica until proved otherwise. A normal or only marginally elevated ESR would make the diagnosis very unlikely. There are no specific diagnostic tests. Biopsy of the temporal artery is invariably performed when symptoms or signs suggest scalp vessel inflammation. A careful search under the microscope may be necessary to reveal inflammation of the vessel walls and the presence of giant cells is characteristic. Biopsy of the temporal artery is worthwhile in those who exhibit only muscle symptoms since a proportion will display the histopathology of temporal arteritis. When positive, this may conclusively establish the diagnosis in those few cases where uncertainty exists. However, not all doctors consider this procedure to be mandatory when symptoms are confined to the muscles.

Treatment

Once the diagnosis of polymyalgia or temporal arteritis has been made, prompt treatment with corticosteroids is essential. Although the risk of blindness is remote, it is sufficient to warrant urgent treatment. Blindness has been documented in patients with polymyalgia rheumatica and no clinical evidence of temporal arteritis. The disease usually remits after one to several years but treatment is necessary throughout this period. Muscle symptoms respond dramatically to steroid therapy and the ESR usually declines rapidly. A failure to respond is so unusual that the diagnosis may require reconsideration in this event.

8

Infective Arthritis

R. Grahame

Involvement of joints by pathogenic microorganisms occurs in a wide range of infections caused by viruses, bacteria and fungi. In most cases the organisms gain access to the joint via the blood stream, but occasionally direct spread may occur from adjacent osteomyelitis or infection can be introduced as a result of a penetrating wound, or inadvertently at the time of surgery or joint aspiration.

Viral infections

A widespread symmetrical polyarthritis may be seen in the course of rubella, usually occurring as the rash starts to fade. It is usually a shortlived affair settling spontaneously in a few days without sequelae. A similar condition may also occur with rubella immunization. Arthritis is occasionally seen in mumps, chickenpox, smallpox, infectious mononucleosis and infective hepatitis.

Bacterial arthritis

Bacterial arthritis may occur in infections with staphylococcus, streptococcus, gonococcus, meningococcus, pneumococcus, coliform bacillus, salmonella, haemophilus influenzae and brucellosis. Bacteraemia of any cause may result in the development of bacterial infection in one or more synovial joints. This is not surprising since the closed synovial cavity is an ideal culture medium for pathogenic bacteria. Bacterial (pyogenic) arthritis may thus occur in the wake of uncontrolled infection occurring in the respiratory, genitourinary or intestinal tracts. In some patients the focus of infection may be an abscess in the skin, lymph nodes or viscera; or in the case of bacterial endocarditis, on the heart valves. The presence of pathogenic bacteria within the joint leads to a rapid and irreversible destruction of the delicate articular structures, including the articular cartilage (Fig. 8.1). Although this is always a serious disease the pace of joint destruction will depend on the virulence of the offending organism. A joint which has previously been the site of disease or which is currently involved in inflammatory joint disease of any kind is particularly vulnerable to this complication. It is thus a not infrequent complication of rheumatoid arthritis, particularly when the patient's protective immune mechanisms have been dampened by corticosteroid therapy.

Arthritis occurring in patients with infectious diseases is not

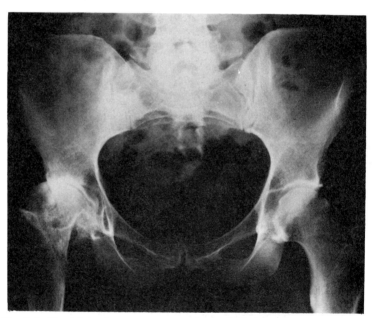

Fig. 8.1. The pelvis of a young woman who in childhood suffered from pyogenic arthritis of the right hip causing total destruction of that joint. She has walked with a limp since that time.

always occasioned by pathogenic bacteria within the joint. The arthritis of Reiter's syndrome which follows non-specific urethritis is a case in point. Another example is the reactive arthritis seen in patients carrying the histocompatibility antigen HLA-B27, who are suffering from enteric infections (see Chapter 6).

Tuberculous arthritis

In the days when bovine tuberculosis was endemic, tuberculous infections of bone and joint were not uncommon in the United Kingdom. They were seen predominantly in the spine (Pott's disease, Fig. 8.2) or in the larger peripheral joints, notably the hip or knee. Characteristically, this is a one-joint disease with swelling and stiffness predominating whilst pain is relatively mild. Unlike other forms of bacterial infection the signs of joint inflammation are less in evidence. Despite this the condition is savagely destructive to the joint if untreated.

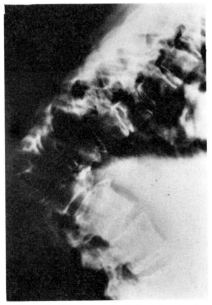

Fig. 8.2. Lateral radiograph of the spine of a patient previously suffering from tuberculosis of the spine (Pott's disease). Note the angular kyphosis.

Although tuberculous disease has become a comparative rarity
in this country, it should be remembered that this is not the
case in other parts of the world, e.g. parts of Asia and Africa
where the disease is endemic. Even in the United Kingdom
cases of joint tuberculosis do occur.

Diagnosis

The most important factor in the diagnosis of infective arthritis
is an awareness of the possibility of its presence. A single
inflamed joint that is not immediately explicable on other
grounds should always be suspected of being infected until
proved otherwise. Pyogenic and tuberculous arthritis are both
eminently treatable diseases, yet if their diagnosis is overlooked
and they remain untreated, serious and irremediable joint
damage may occur. It follows that no effort should be spared
to substantiate or exclude the correct diagnosis in such cases. A
patient with a pre-existing polyarthritis should be suspected of
suffering from secondary bacterial infection if any one joint
appears to be more actively inflamed than the rest. The history
of a recent intra-articular steroid injection in that joint makes
this eventuality highly probable. The presence of fever, inflammation of the regional lymph glands and a polymorphonuclear
leukocytosis in the peripheral blood all point to this diagnosis,
but they may be absent particularly in elderly or debilitated
subjects. Identification of pathogenic bacteria in blood cultures
is further circumstantial evidence pointing to this diagnosis.

  However, confirmatory evidence can only be achieved by the
positive identification of pathogenic bacteria from fluid
obtained from the infected joint. It follows that under these
circumstances aspiration of the joint and collection of synovial
fluid for careful bacteriological analysis is mandatory. It
should, however, be stated that positive cultures are not always
forthcoming when the patient may have received antibiotic
therapy prior to referral. On some occasions it is necessary to
perform repeated synovial fluid examinations, or even culture
specimens of synovial membrane (obtained by closed needle
biopsy) before establishing a positive diagnosis. Where tuberculosis is suspected, biopsy of synovial membrane and exami-

lation both by histopathological and bacteriological means is required. For this purpose it is preferable to obtain material taken by visualization of the joint either by arthroscopy (where this is practicable as in the knee) or by open surgical arthrotomy.

Management

Arthritis occurring in the course of a virus infection requires no specific measures apart from symptomatic treatment with antirheumatic drugs for the relief of pain and stiffness.

Bacterial arthritis requires prompt and thorough antibiotic therapy. The choice of antibiotics will depend ultimately on the results of sensitivity testing performed in the laboratory after the organism has been identified. Since this information is not immediately available, antibiotic therapy should be instituted as soon as the joint has been aspirated and the fluid transported to the laboratory. For this interim period a broad spectrum antibiotic should be chosen, bearing in mind any history of any previous drug allergy that the patient may have experienced. During the initial phases of treatment it is wise to administer antibiotics systemically (either intravenously or intramuscularly), since the oral route may not provide adequate bactericidal levels of the drug.

Drainage of the joint should be carried out at daily intervals by aspirating as much of the purulent synovial fluid as possible. This procedure permits additional antibiotic to be injected directly into the joint. Since the infected synovial cavity is a closed space this form of drainage is an important adjunct to treatment.

Only if thorough antibiotic treatment and repeated aspiration fail should surgical drainage be undertaken. Surgical drainage involves an arthrotomy and insertion of a drain to permit effective removal of the synovial exudate. '

Tuberculous arthritis is nowadays treated primarily by the administration of antituberculous drugs, the role of surgery having been relegated to the occasional arthrodesis or subsequent replacement of affected joints.

9

Crystal Arthritis

T. J. Gibson

The deposition of crystals within a joint can cause pronounced inflammation. Two major forms of arthritis can be ascribed to this mechanism, namely gout and pseudogout. The former is due to crystals of monosodium urate, the latter to those of calcium pyrophosphate. There is some evidence that mild inflammation in what otherwise appears to be osteoarthrosis is provoked by crystals of calcium hydroxyapatite. The significance of these last-mentioned crystals within the joint has not been finally established. Hydroxyapatite deposition in soft tissues such as the subacromial bursa or supraspinatus tendon may be associated with episodes of marked extra-articular inflammation (see p. 25 and Fig. 4.2).

Gout

Gout has been a recognized disease for many centuries. The crystals of urate which deposit in the joints occur in response to elevation of the blood uric acid level. Hyperuricaemia does not invariably lead to gout. For reasons which are uncertain, blood uric acid is higher in men than in women although the levels in postmenopausal women tend to rise and approximate those of men. Not surprisingly, therefore, gout is very much more common in men.

Several factors are known to influence blood uric acid which is a waste product excreted largely by the kidney. It is derived mainly from the breakdown of purines which are essential components of the nucleoprotein found in all living cells. There are two major sources, namely, the breakdown of cells during normal body repair, and the diet. Certain foods such as liver and kidney are especially rich in purines. When cell turnover is greatly accentuated as in leukaemia, the amount of uric acid excreted is very much increased. In this situation blood uric acid may rise and if gout ensues it is termed secondary gout. Another cause of secondary gout is the hyperuricaemia induced by diuretic therapy or other drugs.

Most often, gout cannot be ascribed to another disease. There are probably several causes of the hyperuricaemia associated with primary gout. Some patients may produce too much endogenous uric acid. Very rarely this can be attributed to a definite enzyme defect. Others are unable to excrete uric acid efficiently. Some appear to exhibit evidence of both urate overproduction and a relative impairment of kidney excretion. Other factors which contribute to hyperuricaemia are obesity and excessive alcohol consumption (Fig. 9.1). Some patients

Fig. 9.1. The typical patient with gout is obese and overindulges in alcohol. The site most commonly affected is the first metatarsophalangeal joint.

have a family history of gout. There is an association of gout with hypertension, hypertriglyceridaemia and kidney stones.

Symptoms and signs

The first attack of gouty arthritis usually affects one joint. Most commonly this is the first metatarsophalangeal joint (podagra). It may be precipitated by rapid fluctuations of blood uric acid levels such as may result from dietary indiscretion. Other precipitating factors are intercurrent illness, surgery or local trauma.

The acute arthritis, although excruciatingly painful, is self-limiting and tends to resolve spontaneously over a period of days. A typical history is characterized by recurrent episodes of acute arthritis over a period of months or years. Those with a long history may develop chronic arthritis associated with low grade inflammation and progressive deformities. Uric acid may accumulate within the joint to form tophi. These tophaceous deposits may accumulate visibly on the ear lobes, at the elbows, on the toes (Fig. 9.2), or elsewhere. The chalky crystalline material may periodically ulcerate.

Investigation

The diagnosis can be readily established by examining synovial fluid under the polarizing microscope. Typical monosodium urate crystals will be apparent, many having been ingested by white cells. When a joint effusion is not obtainable, a presumptive diagnosis can be made on the basis of a typical history associated with hyperuricaemia.

X-rays are of limited value except in longstanding cases. Repeated attacks or chronic arthritis will cause loss of articular cartilage. Joint erosions sometimes occur and represent tophaceous deposits within the juxta-articular bone. The erosions may have a 'punched-out' appearance (Fig. 9.2).

Treatment

Management of the acute arthritis includes simple rest and when necessary, splintage. Joint aspiration is in itself helpful.

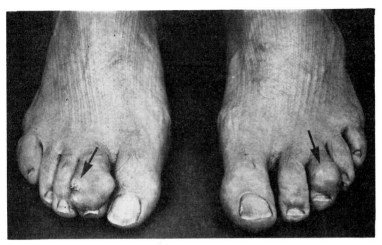

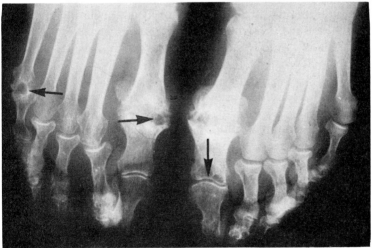

Fig. 9.2. The feet of a patient with chronic tophaceous gout. (above) Large deposits of uric acid have formed ulcerating tophi (→) on his toes. (below) The uric acid deposits have caused joint erosions and cysts, some of which have a 'punched-out' appearance (→).

Colchicine is a drug with a specific action in gout but it has been largely replaced by indomethacin and phenylbutazone.

Resolution of the acute arthritis may be followed by treatment of the underlying cause, hyperuricaemia. When secondary to diuretic therapy or other drugs it is worth considering the continued necessity of such treatments.

Obesity or dietary and alcohol excess may be countered by appropriate counselling. Such measures may be all that is required but patient compliance is notoriously difficult. For the majority, drug therapy is required.

The two major hypouricaemic agents employed today are allopurinol and probenecid. The former exerts its effect by interrupting uric acid formation while the latter increases uric acid excretion by the kidneys. Probenecid is not recommended for those who already excrete very large quantities of uric acid (overproducers) nor for those with renal impairment or calculi. During the initial period of treatment, the rapid decline of blood uric acid may precipitate further acute gout. It is therefore necessary to continue colchicine or its alternatives at least until a normal blood uric acid level has been achieved. Treatment with hypouricaemic drugs may need to be continued indefinitely.

The relationship between gout and elevated serum triglyceride levels may predispose gouty subjects to ischaemic heart disease. Fasting lipids should therefore always be estimated in patients with gout. In the majority, hypertriglyceridaemia can be diminished by weight reduction and avoidance of alcohol excess. Hypertension and mild renal impairment in gout may be caused by sustained hyperuricaemia. There is no clear evidence that reduction of blood uric acid prevents deterioration of renal function but treatment of the hyperuricaemia in this setting is obviously prudent.

Pseudogout

Unlike gout, the joint most commonly involved is the knee. Like gout, the arthritis may be precipitated by trauma, other illness or surgery. The disease is more common in the elderly and has no predilection for either sex. Crystals of calcium pyrophosphate, precipitated or released into the joint cavity, provoke an inflammatory response analogous to that of gout. Rarely, there is a family history of pseudogout. Invariably, this crystal disease is associated with calcification of articular cartilage or the menisci of the knee (chondrocalcinosis). Some metabolic disorders such as hyperparathyroidism and haemochromatosis predispose to widespread chondrocalcinosis and the risk of pseudogout is accentuated in these diseases.

Symptoms and signs

The clinical features are those of any acute arthritis. The diagnosis should be suspected when an elderly patient complains of sudden pain and swelling of a knee joint (Fig. 9.3). The involved joint may also be the site of osteoarthrosis and it is common for patients to complain of chronic pain and stiffness

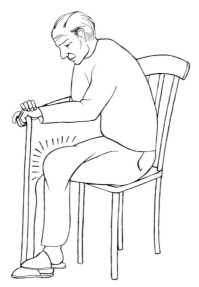

Fig. 9.3. The typical patient with pseudogout is elderly and complains of acute arthritis affecting a knee.

which precedes the acute episode. It is rare for more than one joint to be affected. In addition to the knee, the wrists, elbows and rarely small joints of hands or feet may be involved. Apart from a fever there is little constitutional disturbance.

Investigation

The initial diagnosis is dependent on the demonstration of calcium pyrophosphate crystals within the synovial fluid. These are chunky, rhomboid crystals which exhibit weak positive birefringence under the compensated polarizing microscope. The synovial fluid is inflammatory in nature (see p. 95).

X-rays usually show clear evidence of chondrocalcinosis (Fig. 9.4). This may be a widespread finding involving the symphysis pubis, wrists, hips or other joints. In younger patients with pseudogout and generalized chondrocalcinosis it is important to rule out the possibility of hyperparathyroidism or haemochromatosis. Screening for these diseases may be achieved simply by estimating the serum calcium or iron.

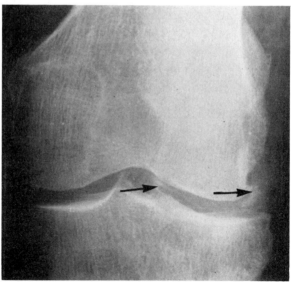

Fig. 9.4. Knee in pseudogout. There is calcification of the lateral meniscus and articular cartilage (↗).

Chondrocalcinosis is a not uncommon finding on X-rays of elderly patients. Its presence does not always denote that acute arthritis is due to pseudogout, thus the importance of examining the synovial fluid. Frequently, articular calcification coexists with the radiological changes of osteoarthrosis and this may be misleading if investigation is confined to an X-ray examination.

Treatment

As with any inflammatory joint disorder rest and splintage are important principles of management. Aspiration of the joint with removal of the offending crystals contributes to the alleviation of pain. The anti-inflammatory drugs, indomethacin and phenylbutazone, are as effective as in gout. Phenylbutazone should be used with caution in elderly patients because its fluid-retaining properties may precipitate heart failure. Colchicine probably has no role in pseudogout.

Recurrent acute attacks of arthritis may well occur but unlike gout, there is usually no fundamental biochemical disturbance which can be treated thus lessening the likelihood of subsequent episodes.

10

The Acutely Inflamed Joint

T. J. Gibson

Acute inflammation of one or more joints is a common problem. Many such cases present to the casualty department but not infrequently it is a condition encountered unexpectedly in patients already in hospital undergoing surgery or other treatment.

There are a number of possible explanations and each can be readily excluded. Most often only one joint is involved. The history and clinical findings may suggest the most likely diagnosis. Joints which are inflamed are warm, sometimes red, tender, swollen and usually contain an effusion.

Trauma

When there is a clear history of injury, a traumatic synovitis, haemarthrosis or mechanical derangement such as a torn meniscus may be suspected. However, an attack of gout may also be provoked by trauma.

Gout

A first attack of gout usually affects only one joint and most often this is the first metatarsophalangeal joint. Sometimes a history of previous episodes spanning several years will be obtained. Several joints may be involved simultaneously. Heavy alcohol consumption, obesity, a family history and the presence of tophi on the ears or elsewhere increase the likelihood of this diagnosis. Gout may be seen for the first time in patients undergoing surgery or after admission for other illness.

Pseudogout

Most often only one joint is involved, usually the knee. Elderly subjects are especially prone. Like gout, this condition may be precipitated by incidental disease or surgical procedures.

Septic arthritis

Septic arthritis occurs more commonly in the elderly and debilitated. A recent history of infection at another site, e.g. pneumonia, might be obtained. Patients with pre-existing rheumatoid arthritis, especially those receiving corticosteroid treatment, are particularly susceptible.

Chronic polyarthritis

Rheumatoid arthritis and other forms of polyarthritis sometimes present as an acute monarthritis. Typical polyarticular features may not become evident for months or even years and the precise diagnosis may remain elusive for much of this time.

Investigation

The single most important investigation of acute arthritis is examination of synovial fluid. Unfortunately this simple procedure is frequently overlooked in the initial stages and treatment may be unnecessarily delayed. When inflamed, even small joints may yield sufficient synovial fluid to establish a diagnosis. The characteristic findings associated with specific diseases are outlined in Table 10.1.

Much information may be obtained from the naked eye appearance of the effusion. A warm tender joint after trauma may contain a large volume of clear fluid with a high viscosity. These are the features of synovial fluid when the underlying

Table 10.1. Characteristics of synovial fluid in various joint disorders

Joint disorder	Appearance	Viscosity	White cell count (per mm³)	Wet or stained smear
Gout	Turbid	Reduced	>2000	Monosodium urate crystals
Pseudogout	Turbid	Reduced	>2000	Calcium pyrophosphate crystals
Sepsis	Purulent	Reduced	>2000 (usually >50 000)	Bacteria
Trauma	Clear or bloodstained	High	<2000	0
Chronic inflammatory disorder	Turbid	Reduced	>2000	0
Osteoarthrosis	Clear	High	<2000	0

problem is not primarily due to inflammation of the synovium. A mechanical derangement such as a torn cartilage or a loose fragment of bone would produce this picture. A very hot joint following trauma may be due to bleeding within the joint cavity and aspiration of blood not only establishes the diagnosis but is therapeutic.

Pronounced inflammation of the synovium results in synovial fluid which is less viscous and more turbid. The opacity of the aspirate is largely dependent on the number of white cells present. In gout, pseudogout and in the acute presentation of chronic polyarthritis the turbidity of the fluid varies from slight to almost purulent. In septic arthritis, obvious pus will usually be obtained.

Further evaluation can be obtained by examination of synovial fluid under the microscope. The crystals of monosodium urate and calcium pyrophosphate which are found in gout and pseudogout respectively may be visualized with an ordinary light microscope. Many of the crystals may be seen lying within white cells. Urate crystals tend to be slender and needle-shaped. By contrast, those of calcium pyrophosphate are oblong or chunky. However, the morphological appearance of the crystals does not allow reliable distinction. The

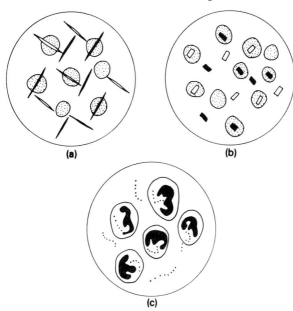

Fig. 10.1. Under the compensated polarizing microscope crystals may be identified as (a) monosodium urate or (b) calcium pyrophosphate. The crystals may be ingested by white cells. They each tend to have a distinct shape and exhibit opposite birefringent properties. On a stained slide, infectious organisms may be identified (c).

availability of a compensated polarizing microscope offers an opportunity to identify the crystals with greater certainty (Fig. 10.1). Those of calcium pyrophosphate show so-called weak positive birefringence whereas those of monosodium urate are negatively birefringent.

A white cell count of the synovial fluid is useful documentary evidence and is particularly valuable when distinguishing inflammatory from non-inflammatory joint disorders. A total count of less than $1000/mm^3$ is likely to indicate the latter whereas one of more than $2000/mm^3$ implies inflammation. When a count falls between these values, a stained smear will indicate whether the predominant white cells are poly-morphonuclear. This would suggest primary joint inflam-mation and a predominance of mononuclear cells would imply the converse. Fluid which is frankly purulent or very turbid should be stained for organisms. The aspiration of pus is not always associated with readily recognizable bacteria on Gram-staining of the fluid. In this situation and in the absence of crystals, antibiotic treatment is justifiable on the assumption of joint infection. Turbid synovial fluid should always be cultured for organisms.

Other diagnostic measures are not likely to prove as conclusive as synovial fluid analysis. X-rays may be normal. Calcification of articular cartilage or the menisci (chondrocalcinosis) may heighten suspicion of pseudogout. This finding is common in the elderly and may therefore be incidental. Subsequent X-ray assessment of obvious traumatic knee effusions may include an arthrogram. This may demonstrate the presence of a torn meniscus.

Further investigation such as an ESR estimation may confirm the inflammatory basis of the arthropathy and a positive test for rheumatoid factor may distinguish the patient with acute onset of rheumatoid arthritis. Blood uric acid determination may help. When elevated it may assist diagnosis in those cases of gout where synovial fluid is not examined.

When the diagnosis remains obscure, biopsy of the synovium may occasionally be helpful. In general, synovial biopsy specimens tend to confirm the impression gained from previous investigations. The synovium may be hypertrophied and infiltrated with chronic inflammatory cells when an inflammatory joint disorder underlies the arthritis. However, there is no certain way of distinguishing the various inflammatory conditions by this means since the changes are essentially similar whatever the precise diagnosis. Biopsy is justifiable because occasionally light microscopy reveals more specific changes such as those of tuberculous infection or villonodular synovitis. Non-inflammatory joint disorders are characterized by normal or merely hypertrophied synovium without inflammatory cells. Biopsies are usually performed by a special needle introduced under local anaesthetic.

Arthroscopy is especially helpful in recognizing mechanical derangements of the knee. This tool is increasingly employed by orthopaedic surgeons who may establish the presence or absence of a lesion without opening the joint cavity. Arthroscopy can visualize all areas of the joint. General anaesthesia is necessary to allow ready manipulation of the instrument within the knee. Under local anaesthesia a restricted but still adequate view may be obtained. Like synovial biopsy, arthroscopy of inflammatory joint conditions often yields disappointingly little information beyond that already acquired by other means. It has the advantage of allowing biopsy of synovium under direct vision.

11

Drug Treatment of the Rheumatic Diseases

April Kay

There are many different rheumatic diseases but pain is a feature common to them all and may persist for months or even years. The number of antirheumatic drugs available reflects the fact that none are curative; they act either by relieving pain or by suppressing the disease process. Patients benefit from the increasing diversity of available drugs but the frequency of side effects, occasionally fatal, is causing increasing concern.

General principles

Pain relief

Many rheumatic patients, particularly those with rheumatoid arthritis, are in some pain most of the time. Control of chronic pain excludes the use of addictive drugs, such as narcotic analgesics, except in the management of superimposed acute episodes. It is difficult to find a drug regime which will provide consistent relief of pain on a continuous basis over weeks or months. Careful adjustment of dosage and timing of administration, suited to the individual patient, help to give optimum relief. It may be necessary to focus analgesic and anti-inflammatory treatment to give maximum relief either

Table 11.1. Analgesic and anti-inflammatory drugs commonly used in the treatment of rheumatic diseases

Approved name	Proprietary name	Presentation	Usual dose	Frequency
*alclofenac	Prinalgin	capsule	500–1000 mg	1–3 times daily
*aloxiprin	Palaprin Forte	tablet	600–900 mg	1–3 times daily
aspirin	Disprin/Solprin	soluble tablet	300–900 mg	up to 4 hourly
	Claradin	effervescent tablet	300–900 mg	up to 4 hourly
	Nuseal	enteric-coated tablet	325–975 mg	up to 4 hourly
	Levius	sustained release tablet	500–1000 mg	up to 4 hourly
*benorylate	Benoral	tablet	750 mg	3 times daily
		suspension	5–10 ml	2–3 times daily
dextropopoxyphene hydrochloride and paracetamol	Distalgesic	tablet	2 tablets	3–4 times daily
dihydrocodeine	DF118	tablet	30–60 mg	up to 4 hourly
*ibuprofen	Brufen	tablet	200–400 mg	2–4 times daily
*indomethacin	Indocid	capsule	25–75 mg	3 times daily
		suppository	100 mg	once or twice nightly
*ketoprofen	Orudis/Alrheumat	capsule	50 mg	3 times daily
*naproxen	Naprosyn	tablet	250 mg	twice daily
		suspension	10 ml	twice daily
*oxyphenbutazone	Tanderil/Tandacote	tablet	100 mg	1–3 times daily
	Tanderil	suppository	250 mg	once nightly
paracetamol	Panadol/Panasorb	tablet	500–1000 mg	up to 4 hourly
*phenylbutazone	Butacote/Butazolidin	tablet	100–200 mg	1–3 times daily
	Butazolidin	suppository	250 mg	once nightly
		injection	200–600 mg	less than daily

* Non-steroid anti-inflammatory drugs.

when most physical activity has to be undertaken or to combat
night pain. Pain due to an inflammatory process, such as joint
synovitis, will most probably be relieved by anti-inflammatory
drugs but if discomfort is secondary to mechanical changes in
an already destroyed joint, analgesics may be more helpful
(Table 11.1).

Night drugs

Joint and muscle pain are often most troublesome at night,
because of body position, movement in sleep, pressure from
bedclothes, redistribution of body fluids or diurnal variations
of hormone levels. Also, pain is less well tolerated at night
when it prevents sleep and diversions are few. Hypnotic drugs,
given alone, sometimes make matters worse by reducing
normal sleep movements so that the patient is stiffer than usual
on waking. A combination of a sedative and an anti-
inflammatory drug is often satisfactory; rheumatoid patients
are particularly helped by diazepam 5–10 mg with indomethacin 50 mg. Another useful combination can be nitrazepam 5–
10 mg and enteric-coated aspirin up to 975 mg taken last thing
at night. Night cramp is another cause of disturbed sleep in the
arthritic patient; quinine sulphate 200–400 mg will usually give
relief.

Antidepressive drugs

Patients with pain and disabling locomotor disease, not
surprisingly, often become depressed. Exhaustion from coping
with the pain and the resultant lack of sleep or loneliness and
the many other social problems faced by rheumatic patients
can all contribute to the depression. Imipramine or amitriptyl-
ine are helpful but their use is complementary to the optimum
management of the rheumatic complaint. It is particularly
important not to ascribe an increase in the patient's symptoms
to depression or anxiety when the cause is organic and should
be treated in its own right.

Drugs during pregnancy

As few antirheumatic drugs as possible should be given during pregnancy. Suspicion of teratogenicity has even been raised against aspirin but the evidence is uncertain. Young rheumatoid patients must be encouraged to discuss their plans for pregnancy so that unsuitable drugs can be stopped in time; any teratogenic effect will happen very early, often before pregnancy is confirmed. Fortunately most rheumatoid patients go into remission during pregnancy, as a result of hormonal changes, and so the need for drugs is diminished.

Rheumatoid arthritis

The symptoms of active rheumatoid arthritis are due mostly to inflamed and hypertrophied synovium lining joints and surrounding tendons; but patients may also be generally unwell and are often anaemic.

Attitudes to the drug treatment of rheumatoid disease vary widely. Some rheumatologists favour a conservative approach using only analgesic and anti-inflammatory drugs, except in severe cases. Another point of view is that an attempt should be made to control the disease as early as possible, before the joints are irreversibly damaged. The drugs which can be used to control the disease (Table 11.2), although effective, all have potential hazards.

Aspirin

For many years aspirin, with both an analgesic and an anti-inflammatory effect, has been the mainstay of the first line management of rheumatoid disease. The effectiveness of salicylate depends on achieving and maintaining adequate blood levels which may be impossible without causing tinnitus or nausea. Using an enteric-coated preparation, which passes intact through the stomach, will reduce gastrointestinal distur-

Table 11.2. **Drugs for the treatment of rheumatoid arthritis**

Approved name	Proprietary name	Usual dose
sodium aurothiomalate	Myocrisin	10–50 mg/week
D-penicillamine	Distamine	125–750 mg/day
hydroxychloroquine sulphate	Plaquenil	200–400 mg/day
prednisone/prednisolone	Decortisyl/Precortisyl	5–10 mg/day
azathioprine	Imuran	50–150 mg/day
cyclophosphamide	Endoxana	up to 2 mg/kg body weight/day
chlorambucil	Leukeran	0.2 mg/kg body weight/day

bance. There is good absorption from the small intestine about six hours after ingestion, so that dosing can be timed to ensure adequate salicylate levels when needed, for example on waking in the morning.

Non-steroid anti-inflammatory drugs

The non-steroid anti-inflammatory drugs have partly replaced aspirin although they are not always more effective; there are a large and increasing number of these drugs, and the most commonly used are shown in Table 11.1. Unfortunately these preparations are associated with a high frequency of adverse reactions particularly affecting the gastrointestinal tract. The choice of a non-steroid anti-inflammatory drug for a particular patient may, in practice, depend on its acceptability rather than its effectiveness. Indomethacin, probably the most popular and effective of these drugs in the treatment of rheumatoid arthritis, can be given either as a capsule or a suppository. Nausea and headaches unfortunately occur frequently, making the drug unacceptable to a proportion of patients. Serious adverse reactions to indomethacin are rare.

Steroids

Corticosteroids (Table 11.3) have a powerful anti-inflammatory action similar to that of steroids naturally produced by the adrenal cortex. Corticosteroids were first used

Table 11.3. Corticosteroids and adrenocortical stimulating drugs

Approved name	Proprietary name	Presentation	Usual dose	Frequency
prednisone	Decortisyl/Deltacortone	tablet	5 mg	once or twice daily
prednisolone	Precortisyl/Delta-Cortef/Codelcortone	tablet	5 mg	once or twice daily
		enteric-coated tablet	5 mg	once or twice daily
prednisolone mono-sodium phosphate	Prednesol	effervescent tablet	5 mg	once or twice daily
methylprednisolone	Medrone	tablet	4 mg	once or twice daily
	Medrone Medules	capsule	4 mg	once or twice daily
hydrocortisone acetate	Cortistab	intra-articular or intramuscular injection	25–50 mg	as required
methylprednisolone	Depo-medrone	intra-articular or intramuscular injection	40 mg	as required
triamcinolone hexacetonide	Lederspan	intra-articular injection	20 mg	as required
ACTH (corticotrophin)	Acthar Gel	intramuscular injection	20–40 units	up to once daily
tetracosactrin acetate	Synacthen depot	intramuscular injection	0.25–1 mg	2–3 times weekly
hydrocortisone sodium succinate	Sola-Cortef	intravenous injection	100 mg	as required

in the treatment of rheumatoid arthritis in about 1950. The effect was dramatic and with large doses almost complete suppression of the disease could be achieved. Optimists thought that a cure for rheumatoid arthritis had at last been found but as time went by the long-term complications became apparent: osteoporosis, peptic ulceration and hypertension, to name but a few. Another serious sequel to prolonged corticosteroid treatment is suppression of the normal adrenal cortical function which is related both to dosage and duration of treatment. Patients who have been on as little as 7.5 mg prednisone per day for more than a few months may be unable to increase their natural secretion of corticosteroids as part of the normal response to stress. Supplementary corticosteroid must therefore be given to these patients for up to two years after ceasing treatment with these drugs. If the patient is undergoing surgery or has an intercurrent illness a supplementary dose of corticosteroid should be given. As adrenal insufficiency often presents with nausea and vomiting it is better to give the supplement by the intramuscular or intravenous route.

Systemic corticosteroids are now less popular than they were in the treatment of rheumatoid arthritis but should not altogether be discarded. A patient with acute rheumatoid arthritis can be relieved of pain and malaise while slow-acting drugs, such as gold and D-penicillamine, take effect. As the patient goes into remission the corticosteroid dose is reduced and eventually withdrawn altogether. Prednisone 5 mg/day given to relieve symptoms at the period of maximum severity can be useful and causes little trouble, and if given at night will prevent early morning stiffness. ACTH or tetracosactrin acetate (Table 11.3), which stimulates the adrenals to produce natural corticosteroids and does not suppress their function, may be preferred.

Local treatment of active rheumatoid joints by injection of corticosteroid can be very effective, particularly when only a few joints are involved. Hydrocortisone acetate or other longer-acting corticosteroids, such as triamcinolone hexacetonide (Table 11.3) are introduced with or without a local anaesthetic. A proportion of the corticosteroid is absorbed into the blood stream and will have a systemic effect.

Slow-acting drugs

There are few drugs which are known to slow the progression of rheumatoid arthritis; gold, D-penicillamine and antimalarials induce remission in a proportion of patients. It is thought that these drugs act by modifying the immune response; they do not produce immediate relief and can cause serious adverse effects.

Gold. Gold has been used in the treatment of rheumatoid arthritis for about fifty years. It was first found to be effective when under trial as an antituberculous agent. It is usually administered as sodium aurothiomalate given by weekly intramuscular injections starting with a test dose of 10 mg and proceeding to a weekly dose of 20–50 mg. Response is seldom apparent before a total dose of 300 mg has been given and may depend on achieving an adequate tissue level of gold. Once remission is induced disease suppression can be maintained using less frequent or smaller doses. Recommended regimes vary but opinion is moving towards lower and more flexible dose schedules. Gold is effective in the majority of rheumatoid patients who can tolerate it but in up to one-third of patients it has to be withdrawn because of side effects. Skin rashes are common both early and late in treatment; mouth ulcers, proteinuria and blood abnormalities are also important problems (see Adverse reactions, p. 108).

D-*penicillamine.* D-penicillamine, a drug more recently introduced for the treatment of rheumatoid arthritis, is in many ways comparable to gold. The advantage of D-penicillamine over gold is that it can be given by mouth. Patients are usually started on a dose of 125–250 mg/day and this is gradually increased over a period of several months up to 750 mg/day. Adverse reactions are frequent and potentially serious and, as with gold, include rashes, renal damage and blood dyscrasias.

More rarely patients on D-penicillamine develop muscle weakness similar to myasthenia gravis.

Antimalarials. The antimalarials, chloroquine sulphate and hydroxychloroquine sulphate, are used in the treatment of rheumatoid arthritis with good results. Daily doses of 200 or 250 mg will, if effective, usually lead to remission in about three months, and can be maintained by less frequent or smaller doses of the drug. Chloroquine compounds accumulate in certain tissues, particularly the eye. It is mandatory to include ophthalmic assessments in the management of rheumatoid patients on chloroquine derivatives (see Adverse reactions, p. 108).

Cytostatic drugs

In some cases of severe progressive rheumatoid arthritis, none of the drugs so far mentioned controls the disease and it may then be justified to consider submitting patients to more hazardous forms of treatment in order to improve the quality of life for them. Cytostatic drugs, commonly used in the treatment of malignant diseases, are effective, singly or in combination, at suppressing most cases of unremitting rheumatoid disease. Cyclophosphamide, azathioprine and chlorambucil have all been used successfully in some cases. Administration has to be most carefully supervised for the immediate toxic effects, particularly on the bone marrow (see Adverse reactions, p. 108). These drugs are not used more often not only because of immediate dangers but also because evidence suggests that their use may be associated with the later development of malignant diseases, particularly lymphomas.

Anthelmintic drugs

Recently it has been suggested that anthelmintic drugs, such as levamisole, may be effective in rheumatoid arthritis as modulators of the immune response. It is not yet clear whether the benefits from levamisole will outweigh the risks of adverse reactions.

Iron

The anaemia of rheumatoid arthritis is complicated and although the blood picture may suggest iron deficiency in most cases it is due to sequestration of iron in the tissues. It is debatable whether or not iron supplements are either necessary or helpful; the anaemia tends to resolve as remission of rheumatoid arthritis is induced or develops spontaneously. Iron impairs the absorption of D-penicillamine; if a patient is on both drugs, at least two hours should be allowed to elapse after taking D-penicillamine before iron is given.

Osteoarthrosis

Osteoarthrosis, by far the most common of the rheumatic disorders, is often not very amenable to drug treatment. Weight-bearing joints, especially hips and knees, are frequently involved. Non-steroid anti-inflammatory drugs are sometimes helpful in early cases, supporting the recent suggestion that there may be an inflammatory basis to what has previously been regarded as a degenerative condition. Indomethacin, for example, is particularly helpful in relieving the pain in osteoarthrosis of the hip.

Drugs offer little relief in advanced osteoarthrosis when pain is due to the abnormal mechanics of the joint with opposing bone ends denuded of normal cartilage and with exuberant bony overgrowth. Analgesics give only partial and intermittent pain relief to a condition which is increasingly becoming the province of the orthopaedic surgeon.

Ankylosing spondylitis

During the active stage of ankylosing spondylitis when pain and stiffness are present it is important to maintain as much movement as possible, particularly in the commonly affected spinal and proximal limb joints. Exercises to maintain movement are better carried out if pain and stiffness are suppressed.

Phenylbutazone is an effective drug in the treatment of ankylosing spondylitis, so much so that when the diagnosis is in doubt a good response to phenylbutazone is regarded as supportive evidence. Recently it has been suggested that apart from suppressing pain phenylbutazone may modify the progress of the disease, thus making it worthwhile to continue the drug at low dosage, e.g. 100 mg/day even when the disease is apparently inactive. The disadvantage of phenylbutazone (and oxyphenbutazone) is that it occasionally causes thrombocytopenia or aplastic anaemia, and for this reason some prefer to use other anti-inflammatory preparations such as indomethacin.

Temporal arteritis and polymyalgia rheumatica

Temporal arteritis and polymyalgia rheumatica are overlapping conditions which both occur in elderly patients. Untreated temporal arteritis may result in sudden blindness. Non-steroid anti-inflammatory drugs can suppress the headache and scalp tenderness of temporal arteritis without lessening the risk of occlusion of the ophthalmic artery, thus giving a false sense of security. Corticosteroids, in dosage adequate to suppress symptoms and lower the sedimentation rate, will prevent blindness. It may be necessary to use a dose of prednisone as high as 60 mg/day in the acute phase, but within a few weeks it should be possible to lower the dose of prednisone to a more acceptable level. The maintenance dose of prednisone must be frequently adjusted in response to disease activity, and kept as low as possible as corticosteroid treatment may have to be continued for several years.

Adverse reactions and drug monitoring

The drug treatment of rheumatic conditions, particularly rheumatoid arthritis and other inflammatory arthritides, has become more sophisticated. Unfortunately drugs act not only on the disease process but also on other processes in the body, sometimes producing adverse reactions. There may be only a narrow margin between the effective and the toxic dose of a drug, or side effects may be unpredictable and unrelated to the dosage. Monitoring of drug therapy is now an important aspect of the care of rheumatoid patients on gold, D-penicillamine and cytostatic drugs; these patients need very careful supervision.

Blood counts

Aplastic anaemia with destruction of the blood precursors in the bone marrow is the commonest cause of death related to the administration of antirheumatic drugs. This serious complication usually develops gradually and its onset is suggested by a persistent fall in one or all elements of the blood count. Careful and frequent monitoring of sequential blood counts will usually reveal a downward trend before it is irreversible. If the drug is stopped in time the bone marrow will recover without any damage to the patient. Regular blood counts are mandatory in patients on gold, D-penicillamine and cytostatic drugs.

Urine testing

Proteinuria is a useful indicator of early drug damage to the kidney. The glomerular filtrate is concentrated during its passage through the tubule, thus tubular cells are exposed to quite high concentrations of a drug which may damage them and result in a protein leak. Immunological processes may also be involved. Persistent proteinuria in patients on gold and D-penicillamine is a reason for stopping the drug.

ACTH, tetracosactrin acetate and corticosteroids, such as prednisone, may cause glycosuria and in some patients may expose latent diabetes mellitus.

Eye testing

Chloroquine compounds, although generally very safe, accumulate in tissues. In the eye corneal deposition of chloroquine, which may cause blurring of vision, is reversible but excessive deposition in the retina can result in irreversible blindness. Patients on chloroquine must be regularly assessed by an ophthalmologist to make sure that visual acuity is not deteriorating.

Patients receiving large doses of corticosteroids over a long period of time can develop cataracts.

Chest X-ray

Patients receiving corticosteroids over a long period should have periodic chest X-rays as corticosteroids can reactivate old pulmonary tuberculosis.

Skin and mucous membrane

Drugs are a common cause of skin rashes, some of which are transient and harmless whilst others are important indicators of serious complications. An irritating rash occurs in patients on gold (Fig. 11.1); it is usually transient but if treatment is continued, particularly in patients who have been on chrysotherapy for some time, exfoliative dermatitis can develop. Rashes in patients on D-penicillamine may also become serious if they are ignored. A purpuric rash or bruising may be the presenting sign of thrombocytopenia or aplastic anaemia.

Ulceration of the mucous membrane in the mouth is quite common early in the course of gold treatment. Rarely, more extensive ulceration of the gut may present as bloody diarrhoea. Patients with low white blood cell counts due to drugs, such as gold or D-penicillamine, may complain of a sore throat.

Drug interactions

Good drug monitoring requires anticipation of the likely adverse effects associated with each drug; it is also important to consider any possible interactions either between the anti-rheumatic drugs or between one antirheumatic drug and

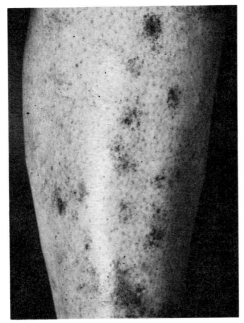

Fig. 11.1. Itchy rash on anterior aspect of the right shin following treatment with gold salts in a patient with rheumatoid arthritis.

another medication which the patient is taking. For example, patients on the anticoagulant warfarin should not be given phenylbutazone which potentiates its effect and may therefore produce bleeding. Some drug interactions are not dangerous but one drug may reduce the effectiveness of the other, for example, iron and D-penicillamine (see p. 107).

Summary

Drugs that cure rheumatic diseases are not yet available but much can be done to relieve pain and suppress disease activity. Small but significant gains for the patient can be achieved by careful attention to the details of drug administration. Many of the most effective drugs are potentially hazardous and their administration must be carefully supervised.

12

Surgery in the Rheumatic Diseases

M. Laurence

The treatment of the patient with polyarthritis would remain incomplete but for the contribution that reconstructive surgery can make. The condition presents a great variety of problems which are not only medical and surgical, but social, emotional and economic affecting the patient's family life.

The contribution of surgery will be described in detail later, but first it must be put into context. An operation is no more than an incident in the management of an arthritic; it is a supplement, not an alternative, and its follow-up is as important as the technique. Many patients, of course, never require surgical treatment, but when a patient does, the decision is very much a joint one, and the subsequent management is often complex. The surgeon must be prepared to assume responsibility for the technical procedure, but not necessarily for the decision regarding surgery. He becomes the doctor in charge for the pre-operative period, and the physician withdraws to a secondary position. Similarly, the surgeon directs rehabilitation until such time as the maximum improvement has been obtained from the operation. With regard to medication, both surgeon and physician are fortunate to be able to rely upon the anaesthetist, who accepts control of the first three days. Thereafter, the physician resumes responsibility, but in an efficient unit none of these duties are ever defined. Each clinician is capable of taking the role of another in time of need. We assume we are dealing with an incurable disease, although realizing that many cases resolve spontaneously under conservative treatment. Rheumatic disease, even if it defies cure, should be controllable by means of some or all of the techniques at our disposal.

The surgeon may take part at several stages of the disease process, and of course the point at which he becomes involved depends primarily upon when the sufferer first seeks medical advice. The majority of cases of rheumatoid arthritis present to the rheumatologist with a classical peripheral polyarthritis with appropriate blood changes. On the other hand, a patient may present with localized synovitis, and the diagnosis may not be made; for example, the classical conditions of trigger finger, carpal tunnel, hallux valgus, and de Quervain's tenosynovitis, are usually referred to an orthopaedic clinic. The treatment of each is often considered to be surgical in the first instance and although the proportion of such cases which present subsequent manifestations of rheumatoid disease is small, none the less each presents more commonly in patients about to develop generalized rheumatoid arthritis than in the normal population. This does not alter the surgical indication for treatment, but the surgeon should be suspicious when other parts of the body develop similar or related symptoms before or after the initial lesion has been treated. Monarthritis, affecting the knee commonly, chronic bursitis particularly at the elbow, and synovial herniation, especially from the back of the knee, are also typical ways in which rheumatoid disease can lead a patient to an orthopaedic clinic before the generalized disease is suspected. The second stage in which a surgeon can be involved in the treatment of polyarthritis is to assist a rheumatologist in establishing the diagnosis and excluding infective or other causes for chronic synovitis. In this capacity, the surgeon takes the role of technician and acts at the direction of his colleague, at whose request he performs surgical biopsy of synovium, bone or lymph gland. He may be asked to inspect a knee joint by arthroscopy, although in many units this procedure is efficiently carried out by a physician.

With the diagnosis firmly made the surgeon may be called upon to contribute to the treatment of the arthritic at two stages of the disease process. These can be defined simply as *early* or *late*. The former refers to a stage of synovitis before there has been any physical damage to the organ of movement, before there has been destruction of the articular cartilage or damage to tendons in synovial sheaths. The latter implies that irrevocable destruction has occurred, calling for repair or reconstruction.

Early stage

Let there be no doubt that resolution of the inflammatory process is very much better and more successfully brought about by medical means, but there remains a number of cases that resist such treatment and in whom the synovial granuloma reaches proportions which cannot shrink. The sheer bulk of

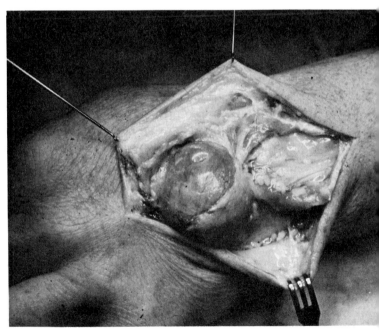

Fig. 12.1. Mass of hypertrophic synovium on the dorsum of the wrist eroding the joint and the extensor tendons running through. Synovectomy, by removing the inflamed tissue, prevents further damage.

ypertrophic synovium leads to its further damage in the course of joint or tendon movement. Physical damage by earing a thickened inflamed synovium perpetuates the inflammation, so that a proportion of cases continue to worsen even hough the primary cause of the disease (whatever it may be) las resolved. The histological appearances in chronic arthritis re not sufficiently specific for one to be sure as to whether nflammation which has become chronic is due primarily to a pecific factor or to traumatic irritation of a hypertrophic ynovitis of any cause. This vicious circle could clearly be roken by the physical removal of the mass of granulation issue, and this principle would explain the many excellent esults that follow early synovectomy (Fig. 12.1). The fact that he primary etiological factor may still be active explains why uch an operative procedure does not always succeed, and the ynovitis sometimes recurs. The decision as to when to perform synovectomy is made on clinical grounds alone. Experience las shown that the operation can be offered with good hope of uccess in certain areas of the body, but not in others.

Good results following synovectomy
  Knee
  Elbow
  Metacarpophalangeal joints
  Tendon sheaths, dorsal aspect wrist
  Tendon sheaths, flexor aspect wrist
  Subdeltoid bursa, shoulder
Poor results following synovectomy
  Interphalangeal joints
  Ankle
  Tarsal joints
  Wrist
  Hip

Knee. The joint proper has a cavernous synovial membrane, and is most easily accessible from an anterior surgical incision, vhen almost all the granulation tissue can be removed. Aftercare is critical because postoperative adhesion between raw urfaces would cause stiffness. Mobility must be re-established before fibrinous adhesion matures to fibrous scarring. If active exercises are not effective, the joint is manipulated unde anaesthetic before three weeks have elapsed.

Arising from the back of the knee joint popliteal bursa present as tense, sometimes painful, swellings which occasion ally rupture and create lakes of synovial fluid in the cal simulating the oedema of deep vein thrombosis. This fluid i the product of the knee joint; any treatment aimed at loca removal of the popliteal or calf cysts must fail as more fluid i pumped out of the back of the knee under valvular force Synovectomy of the joint proper stops the flow at source.

Lesser operations about the knee joint, such as removal o prepatellar bursa or rheumatoid nodules, are done fo convenience rather than because they present any threat to th articulation.

Hand. Rheumatoid synovitis presents in two areas of the hand the joints and the tendon sheaths. It has been stated that mor disability arises from the latter than the former, and this i evident from such minor conditions as trigger finger an carpal tunnel. Granulomatous swellings on the back of th wrist are common too and require surgical removal if functio becomes impaired. Persistent chronic inflammation is destruc tive of tendons as it is of articular cartilage. Surgery i undertaken to relieve pressure on nerves, release obstructe tendons and decompress tightly swollen joints. When thes conditions are complicated by pain, the benefit followin operation is dramatic. As in the knee joint, adhesion is danger and therefore rehabilitation commences early. Man areas of a rheumatoid hand may call for some minor or majo procedure simultaneously, but careful judgement is require not to do more than a hand can tolerate and still recove mobility. Surgical overdosage is very possible when dorsa tendons, joints and flexor tendons are all chronically affected.

Elbow. The elbow joint itself can usually cope with mino disability in the form of limited movement, but chroni swelling and increasing pain would be an indication fo synovectomy. Should joint swelling produce ulnar nerv symptoms, the need for surgery is more pressing. On the othe hand the common lesions of olecranon bursitis and nodules on the point of the elbow may be removed for convenience, usually if some other more pressing lesion elsewhere is being operated upon.

Shoulder, hip and foot. The shoulder, hip and foot are also affected early in rheumatoid arthritis, but are not operated upon at all commonly because the benefit of surgery is not sustained, the symptoms do not warrant it, or the surgery carries unacceptable risks.

Late stage

When the disease process has produced irreversible damage in a joint or tendon sheath, repair or reconstruction is required. Appropriate surgery will be described in detail for each structure, because each presents totally different problems with regard to technique, biomechanics and, in particular, rehabilitation. Broadly, tendon ruptures call for simple repair or transposition of less valuable tendons. Articular damage requires arthrodesis, osteotomy or arthroplasty, either artificial replacement or excision.

Tendon rupture

Typical examples of tendon rupture occur in the extensor tendons on the back of the hand. Most commonly these present as sudden 'paralysis' of extension of the little finger, later the ring and middle finger; this is the order in which the tendons snap. The site of the lesion is at the level of the wrist joint. It has always been thought that the eroded head of ulna is responsible, and it is usual for that bone to be removed at the time of surgical repair. The most important step in the management of the lesion is to make the diagnosis. Too often it is missed and the disability in the fingers is put down to the arthritis in the metacarpophalangeal joints. No amount of physiotherapy will ever recover lost extension due to a ruptured tendon. Surgical repair is effected by suturing the

distal stump to the surviving extensors of adjacent fingers.
Sometimes the index is the only tendon to escape and it can be
used to power all the other fingers.

Rupture of flexor tendons is less common, but when it
happens it is far more difficult to treat. Repair may call for
tendon graft, and careful consideration must be given to the
overall function of the hand before embarking on what is a
very arduous programme of surgery and rehabilitation. The
long head of the biceps, the Achilles tendon, the patellar
tendon or the quadriceps tendon above the knee occasionally
rupture; surgical treatment of each of these must be carefully
judged, bearing in mind the degrees of disability produced by
the lesion, the likelihood of a successful outcome following
operation, and the danger of complications. Many such lesions
are deemed tolerable.

Arthrodesis

Arthrodesis is the solid bony fusion of joints. It sacrifices all
movement in return for absolute stability and is therefore
reserved for specific joints in which stability is vital:

> Intervertebral joints
> Radio-carpal
> First metacarpophalangeal
> Interphalangeal of fingers and toes
> First metatarsophalangeal
> Intertarsal
> Ankle
> Knee

Spine. The most common cause of arthritis in the spine is
degenerative disease. It is seen in both lumbar and cervical
regions. Changes are to be seen radiographically in both the
inter-body joints and the posterior articulations. The spine is a
good example of a multiple series of joints of which one or two
may be badly affected; movement of these can be sacrificed
(indeed it is often already lost) and the adjacent joints relied
upon to provide mobility. Spinal fusion can be performed in

the lumbar or cervical region when one, or at most two, joints are seen to be the cause of the patient's pain.

Precise diagnosis is vital. Mistakes have often been made in the past because joints which seem radiographically to be the worst affected, may not be the joints causing pain. Occasionally it is obvious, as for example in association with spondylolysis (a defect in the pars interarticularis) or in the late results of a particular fracture affecting one vertebral body and its adjacent disc. The spine is affected by rheumatoid disease in decreasing frequency from above downwards. It is to be seen at its worst at the atlantoaxial joint, where granulation tissue erodes the odontoid process, causing instability of that joint. Forward subluxation occurs, and the spinal column is at risk. Some instability is common in advanced rheumatoid arthritis, and X-ray examination is an essential part of the general assessment before any operation in patients suffering from this disease. Anaesthetists are particularly conscious of the danger in moving the neck; not to be able to do so causes serious airway problems. Stability is called for and operations are done to bridge the atlantoaxial joint with bone grafts laid on the posterior arch from the back, or through the pharynx anteriorly. Such surgical procedures are fraught with obvious dangers, and recent experience has led to the acceptance of a certain degree of instability (say 5 or 6 mm), assuming there has been no suggestion that the spinal cord has been compressed or irritated to produce long tract neurological signs.

As everywhere, case selection for surgery is crucial. It would be naive to expect that only one spinal joint might be affected by idiopathic degenerative or rheumatoid disease. Therefore one joint arthrodesed will throw extra stress upon a second similarly affected, and its state of disease would rapidly advance to be as bad as the first. Nevertheless, impending quadriplegia calls for stabilization using bone grafts, supported perhaps by internal wires and a soft collar.

Hand. The joints of the thumb, the interphalangeal joints and the wrist may benefit from stability where erosive disease renders them frail. Obviously there is a limit to the number of joints which can be treated in this way so that even an imperfect

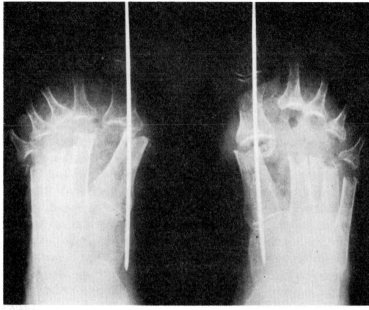

Fig. 12.2. Excision of the heads of the metatarsals in the feet to relieve severe pain. The big toe is being arthrodesed by means of a wire passed through it.

form of arthroplasty is to be preferred for joints adjacent to the stiffened one. The technique of arthrodesis commonly utilizes some form of internal fixation with wires or screws.

Foot. The interphalangeal joints of the toes and the metatarso-phalangeal joint of the hallux have mobility of very limited value. Deformity is more disabling. It may be permanently corrected by arthrodesis, although operations to excise the joints are more commonly employed (Fig. 12.2).

Ankle and knee. The major joints of the leg would be stiffened only if arthroplasty were to fail or be deemed unwise for a variety of reasons.

Osteotomy

Osteotomy is the division of bone ends and their realignment in a new position. It is employed to correct deformity which is casting undue stress upon an arthritic joint which still retains potential function. It is performed at the following sites: knee, first metatarsophalangeal and hip.

Knee. Osteotomy is most commonly used to treat the knee. Valgus or varus angulation is produced by selective erosion of lateral or medial condyles and it cannot be controlled by any muscular action. Body weight will tend to increase the deformity, and after a certain point the convex side will actually open up when weight is taken on the leg. Osteotomy, close to the joint, and sometimes performed on both sides of it (above and below) will correct the angulation and re-distribute the load to relatively undamaged parts of the condylar surfaces.

Historically, intertrochanteric osteotomy of the femur was a standard treatment for degenerative arthritis of the hip joint in the decades leading up to 1960. It was done in a great variety of fashions, producing sometimes valgus and sometimes varus angulation at the site of osteotomy. The beneficial results of this procedure are statistically well documented. However, basic research has failed to provide a convincing explanation, and this was never an operation designed logically from first principles. Clinical observation discovered the fact that patients suffering from degenerative arthritis of the hip joint and who subsequently fractured the trochanteric region of the femur, enjoyed a significant relief of their arthritic symptoms. This observation led to the development of a deliberately inflicted fracture, which in the early stages was left unfixed, and more latterly performed precisely and secured with plates and screws. The operation fell into disuse after 1960, not because of its failure (66 per cent of patients benefitted), but because of the vastly more reliable results obtained by replacement arthro-plasty.

Arthroplasty

Arthroplasty is the fashioning of a new joint in place of one irrevocably damaged by disease. There are two types, replace-ment and excision; the former implies the use of artificial materials in order to recover stable painless movement; the latter is used where stability and strength can be sacrificed in favour of mobility provided by scar tissue between the two bones.

Hip. Let us consider the basic principles of total joint replacement. The concept is a development of partial joint replacement which was done for advanced destructive disease in both hip and knee. Surgical experience showed that the artifical prostheses replacing one side of the joint allowed progressive destruction to occur on the opposite side. A simple metallic femoral head, for example, can be expected to wear through an arthritic acetabulum within three years. The major credit for development of total prosthetic joints must be given to Charnley and McKee. They worked independently, in Wigan and Norwich, on complete hip joints manufactured from different materials. With the passage of time and through several modifications, total replacement of the hip joint has become perhaps the commonest and most successful major operation in the whole of surgery. The principle lies in the fact that painless movement can be provided between artificial components as long as they are securely fixed into each bone. Methylmethacrylate cement is used to fix the prostheses into the cancellous bone of pelvis and femoral shaft. Fixation is made more secure by reducing to a minimum the friction between components, and for this reason, Charnley's materials—stainless steel and high density poly-ethylene—provide the best combination (Fig. 12.3). There have been many modifications of prosthetic design, but none have significantly affected the principle. Providing there is adequate bone into which the implant can be fixed, and allowing that infection can be avoided, the operation is expected to give total relief of pain and restoration of function. Theoretically, the joint is as secure as it ever will be as soon as the patient leaves the operating table. The only anxiety during the postoperative days is that weak or inhibited muscles might allow the components to dislocate and nurses and physiotherapists must therefore ensure that movements are controlled. This is particularly so when the operation has been done from the

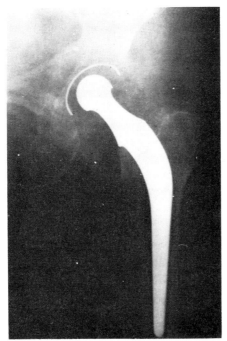

Fig. 12.3. A Charnley low friction arthroplasty of the hip. The metal component is the femoral head and the high-density plastic component is in the acetabulum. (Reproduced by permission of the publishers from E. M. Stone and E. C. Pinney, Orthopaedics for Nurses, 5th ed., Baillière Tindall, 1978.)

posterior aspect. Flexion is then to be strictly curtailed. Standing and walking, however, compress the cement into the cancellous bone more securely and these activities are encouraged from the second or third day.

The principles governing the rehabilitation following total replacement arthroplasty are thus totally different from those used in the general management of the disease before operation. The emphasis on treatment by the therapist is no longer to encourage movement of the hip joint, nor even particularly to strengthen the muscles of the pelvis or leg, but rather in the basic technique of walking, bearing weight on the artificial joint. From this will come confidence and coordination, and movements will return with all the common daily functions of walking and sitting. From a mechanical point of view, the danger to the articulation is from loosening of either component in the bone, and there is a real danger that excessive exercise too early could produce this.

Knee. In the knee joint the problems are different. Prostheses have to provide not only pain-free movement, but also stability against unwanted movements. By contrast with the hip, the knee must move in one plane only and there are no muscles to resist movements of abduction or rotation. Early prosthetic designs were not universally successful, but with the passage of years, great improvements have been made. Again the most successful joints have been fashioned from the same materials as Charnley's hip, metal and plastic. Rigid fixation between the two parts by a metal axle limits the hinge movement too rigidly. Rotatory stress imparted to the bone when the knee is bent causes twisting movements to occur within the shafts of femur and tibia. Fixation between artificial material and bone is lost, and this can cause pain. Later designs have a 'slackness' built into them while stability is provided by the shapes of the components, and the patient's ligaments and muscles. As in the hip, the joint is secure at once, and movement between artificial components is without pain. Rehabilitation is therefore rapid and active movements are encouraged immediately.

Ankle. The ankle is a similar hinge joint, but it is complicated by the fact that rotation occurs at the hind foot between the talus and calcaneum. Often, both the knee and the ankle are severely affected in rheumatoid arthritis; the recovery of movement in one, while the other remains painful and stiff, may be responsible for the indifferent surgical results which are currently being reported. This must be considered an area of experimentation in replacement, but there is no doubt that with the passage of time improved design will give as good results in the foot as have been experienced at the knee and the hip. In front of the ankle the full body weight is not borne, and movements of the toes are not precise. Excision arthroplasty is therefore an adequate solution to problems in the metatarso-phalangeal area, and in the interphalangeal joints.

Hand. Advanced rheumatoid lesions on the joints of the hand raise specific biomechanical problems. No great loads are taken by these joints, but mobility and freedom of pain are essential for function. Use of the hand is always impaired by severe pain and then fairly radical surgical procedures are justified. Through years of experimentation, it has been found that a very simple form of artificial joint, a silastic 'spacer', allows the joint to move while at the same time keeping adjacent bone ends apart. More elaborate and rigid devices have failed. Prosthetic arthroplasty is most effective in replacing the metacarpophalangeal joints; it is not so successful between the phalanges. At the base of the thumb, simple excision arthroplasty (removing the trapezium) gives results which are good enough not to call for more complicated surgery.

Wrist. At the wrist, mobility is less important than stability. Many a hand is rendered useless because the action of finger tendons produces severe pain at the wrist joint, commonly associated with subluxation of the radiocarpal joint. Surgical techniques are therefore limited to stabilizing procedures; arthrodesis, or fibrous ankylosis, gives a satisfactory result. Rotation of the wrist occurs between the lower end of the radius and ulna. Pain in that joint can be relieved by the removal of the lower end of the ulna, and the operation, an excision arthroplasty, carries with it the bonus of removing a potential threat to the extensor tendons of the little finger.

Elbow. At the elbow the head of the radius is relatively disposable, and it can be removed without significantly weakening movement. All redundant synovium and the debris of chronic inflammation can be cleared from the elbow joint at the same operation. The elbow joint proper, the humero-ulnar articulation, is a hinge and all the problems of stability with hinge movements are encountered at the elbow. Synovectomy is the most common operation although the procedure is often done at a stage of the disease when it is unlikely to give a good result. More complicated procedures of joint replacement have so far produced very poor or even disastrous results; but this state of affairs is not to be considered permanent. Many new prostheses, modified in accordance with past experience, are currently being tested and implanted. Doubtless some of them will stand the test of time.

Shoulder. The shoulder joint, although frequently affected by the rheumatoid process and by degenerative conditions of capsule and joint, usually improves with conservative measures. Destruction is occasionally too far advanced, and then it is technically possible to perform an artificial replacement arthroplasty. As with the hip joint, a ball and socket joint is fixed into humerus and scapula respectively so that movements can be resumed instantly but the operation must still be considered as experimental.

With all artificial joints, technical problems constantly present themselves, but one complication from which there is no recovery is infection.

13

Nursing the Rheumatic Patient

J. Beardsley and D. Rowlands

In nursing the rheumatic patient the nurse is called upon to exercise to the full the basic nursing skills which taken together constitute good bedside care. Her patient is often in acute discomfort, sometimes for lengthy periods; improvement is gradual, not dramatic, and the maintenance of morale for both patients and nurses can be psychologically very demanding.

By skilful and gentle handling of the patient during daily nursing procedures and close attention to the support of affected limbs, much can be done to relieve pain and minimize disability.

The commonest disease nursed on a rheumatology ward is undoubtedly rheumatoid arthritis and therefore the nursing management of these patients is of great importance and will be stressed. Other inflammatory joint diseases seen regularly include psoriatic arthritis and ankylosing spondylitis. Among the non-inflammatory joint diseases osteoarthrosis of the knees and hips, and back pain are the commonest.

The successful management of patients with rheumatic diseases depends very much on a team approach. The nurse's role in the team is very important as she is the person who is with the patients continually and who can therefore coordinate with the other members of the team and report back on the patients' progress during different aspects of their treatment. She is there to reiterate and reinforce the advice given by doctors, physiotherapists and occupational therapists and to ensure that patients carry out their treatments regularly and correctly. The nurse on the rheumatology ward is probably not as involved in the actual treatment of patients as she is in other branches of medicine. She thus has more time to concentrate on getting to know her patients and their families. She can talk to them about their worries and problems as well as maintaining their physical comfort and well-being while they are in hospital.

Routine measurements

Temperature, pulse and respiration. Daily measurements of the temperature, pulse and respiration of every patient are made. Patients suffering from a 'flare-up' of rheumatoid arthritis may be pyrexial. In these cases the recordings are made four-hourly.

Blood pressure. The blood pressure is measured on admission only, unless it is raised. Patients on oral steroids have their blood pressure recorded daily.

Grip strengths. Grip strengths of patients suffering from inflammatory joint disease are recorded weekly along with the ESR. These records give a good indication of the degree of activity of the disease and thus its response to hospital treatment.

Urine testing. Urine testing is performed for every patient on admission. Urine is tested weekly for patients on the nephrotoxic drugs such as gold or D-penicillamine. This is occasionally increased to daily if any urinary abnormality is detected.

Weight. Every patient is weighed weekly unless on a special diet, when they are weighed more often. It is a good idea to keep a record of the patient's weight on the ward as loss of weight between admissions is then well documented.

MAIN ASPECTS OF NURSING MANAGEMENT

One of the most important aspects of the nursing management of the rheumatic patient is the maintenance of the *correct position in bed*. This is important in order to prevent deformities which can occur very quickly. The patients themselves also need to be warned of the dangers of bad posture and positioning of limbs so that they can be careful after discharge.

Maintaining the *physical comfort of the patient* is, of course, a priority for any nurse. In patients with chronic disabling diseases, however, their *mental and psychological well-being* is just as important and the nurse must be prepared to spend time getting to know the patients' needs in this respect.

There are certain *specific treatment procedures* carried out on rheumatological wards of which the nurse must be aware. She must be able to assist the doctors with these procedures and to be aware of the effect they can have on the patient.

The nurse is responsible for the administration and monitoring of *drug therapy* which is a vital part of many rheumatic patients' treatment. She must be aware of the implications of the drugs she administers and observe carefully for any side effects. A full discussion of drug therapy was given in Chapter 11.

Correct position in bed and its maintenance

Inflammatory joint disease

The majority of patients admitted to hospital with any type of inflammatory joint disease have to undergo a period of bed rest, the length of time spent in bed depending on the degree of activity of the disease. It is the nurse's responsibility to ensure that patients maintain a correct posture in bed in order to prevent deformities.

Ideally patients should be nursed on a firm mattress with no sagging in the middle. The Kings Fund bed is a suitable model, and its adjustable height is another advantage to both patient and nurse. If this type of bed is not available a fracture board should be placed underneath the mattress to give the necessary support. Most patients prefer to sit up during the day but will in any case need to be in an upright position for eating. Back rests should be firm and the pillows arranged in such a way that the back is kept straight and the neck properly supported. Bed cradles are essential in order to keep the weight of the bedclothes off painful joints and also to enable the patient to carry out any necessary leg exercises while in bed. It is quite common for patients with arthritis badly affecting their knees to place pillows under them to support them comfortably and get some relief from pain. This must not be allowed as it can cause contractures of the knees which may be difficult and time consuming to correct. It may occasionally be necessary to place sandbags at the foot of the bed to keep the patient from slipping down the bed or to prevent footdrop. However, it is more common for plaster of Paris splints to be used for the prevention of deformities such as this. These are usually backslabs held on by Velcro straps or bandages, although more permanent splints are occasionally used. Joints most commonly requiring splints are wrists, knees and ankles. The nurse is not involved in making these splints but it is she who should ensure that they are worn regularly and correctly. Many patients will need help putting splints on and may also need help with eating and washing whilst wearing wrist splints. The nurse must help patients with their splints in order to prevent them being discarded because they are a nuisance. Patients sometimes request a monkey pole at the head of the bed to enable them to lift themselves up. However, these have a limited use as many patients with diseased shoulders and hands are unable to use them.

In contrast, patients with ankylosing spondylitis spend very little time, whilst in hospital, in bed. They carry out a very full physiotherapy programme and are taught the importance of correct posture. The nurse has very little to do for them but once again must stress the importance of all they learn in physiotherapy and encourage them with their exercises.

Non-inflammatory disease

Patients with back disorders also require a firm bed. Many of them also have to spend a period of time on bed rest. They commonly have to lie flat with one pillow only, as any flexion of the neck may distort the lumbar spine as well. Sometimes traction is used for patients suffering from prolapsed intervertebral discs and the nurse should ensure that it is correctly applied. Help with feeding may be needed and drinking straws or feeding beakers should be used so that the patient can maintain a flat position whilst eating.

Patients with osteoarthrosis of the hips or knees are often admitted for a course of physiotherapy. They do not often need to remain on bed rest, but should be warned of the dangers of joint deformities.

Maintenance of physical comfort

Hygiene

As so many rheumatic patients are on bed rest for at least a part of their time in hospital the nurse spends much of her time maintaining their physical comfort and hygiene. This may involve a daily bed bath or assisted wash for each patient whilst he is resting. Care of the hair and nails is also important and the nurse should assist with this if the patient is not able to manage by himself. Special aids are available to help with some of these tasks and if the nurse thinks these might be useful she should discuss the matter with the occupational therapist. The chiropodist should be called in to cut toenails if necessary. Mouth care and care of the teeth is also important. Sometimes if a patient is very disabled he may not be able to visit a dentist whilst at home. Dental treatment while in hospital is then much appreciated. Even when patients are allowed up and about, many will appreciate the offer of a bath or shower. If they are very disabled it may be that they have not enjoyed such a luxury since their last admission to hospital. The morale of the patient is so important on this type of ward that taking a little extra interest in these basic aspects of patient care is very worthwhile. If they are not carried out thoroughly and without undue haste, the patients may feel that they are a nuisance and become resentful of themselves, their condition and the people trying to help them.

Diet and bowels

The patient should be given a balanced, nourishing diet, including plenty of roughage. A large number of patients on bed rest quickly become constipated. Natural bran given each morning with cereals usually has the necessary effect. Many patients will need help to cut up food, and special knives and forks may also be required if the patients' hands are badly affected by disease.

Pressure sores

Prevention. The prevention of pressure sores is another nursing priority when dealing with rheumatic patients on bed rest. In many cases the general physical condition of the patients is not good and therefore sores are more likely to develop. In patients with rheumatoid arthritis the danger is even greater as their skin tends to be thin and atrophic and therefore more easily damaged. The skin over rheumatoid nodules will break down very quickly whilst the patient is confined to bed unless preventive measures are taken.

The only way to prevent sores developing is to maintain regular relief of pressure in any one area. This is not always easy when patients are complaining of stiff and painful joints or when they are immobilized in splints. The nurse must help the patient to change position every few hours. She must also make sure that splints are not rubbing or too tight as this may cause a break in the skin. As mentioned before, she must be scrupulous about hygiene. Damp skin caused by sweating, which may be a problem especially in rheumatoid arthritis, is more at risk of ulcerating. Beds should be kept fresh and clean, crumbs and creases should be regularly removed. Patients should be lifted up carefully and not dragged along the bed.

Many different creams and lotions are used to rub on areas susceptible to developing sores. These can have some value if applied correctly but will not prevent sores unless they are allied with frequent changes of position.

Aids. There are many devices and aids that can be used to reduce pressure and therefore help in the prevention of sores: air-rings for the sacrum and heels, strategically placed foam pads and sheepskin pads for heels and elbows. Very thin and debilitated patients should be nursed lying on sheepskin rugs. Ripple mattresses and, more recently, water beds have been a tremendous help in the prevention of widespread sores in particularly vulnerable patients. A nurse caring for rheumatic patients should be aware of the added danger of pressure sores and should use these aids from the moment the patient is confined to bed. By so doing and by maintaining a high standard of nursing care sores should be prevented.

Treatment. If sores do unfortunately develop, they should be kept clean and dry. In the case of a small, superficial break in the skin, keeping pressure off the area and treating it with a drying agent such as egg white and oxygen should result in healing. For the more extensive necrotic sores a desloughing agent, such as Aserbine, will be required to remove the dead tissue and therefore allow healing to take place. Daily or twice daily dressings will be required depending on the severity of the sore. Once the slough has been removed Eusol can be used for wound packing and to promote general healing. In severe cases plastic surgery may be necessary. It is in these cases that a water bed, if available, can be of value.

Leg ulcers

Leg ulcers are commonly seen on rheumatology wards. Healing can be slow and their treatment may require a prolonged hospital stay. Many leg ulcers follow trauma to the leg, perhaps causing only a small break in the skin at first. Care should obviously be taken while a vulnerable patient is in hospital to try and avoid any damage to the skin which may be caused by splints, bed cradles or wheelchairs. Once an ulcer has developed and hospitalization has been deemed necessary, the patient should be kept on bed rest, preferably with the end of the bed elevated. Swabs should be taken to find out if the ulcer is infected as sometimes systemic antibiotics are required. The ulcer should be dressed regularly, twice a day at first if necessary. Removal of slough is the first priority. This can be achieved with Aserbine cream or hydrogen peroxide. It should then be cleaned with Eusol. Paranet gauze can be used to prevent the dressing from sticking to the ulcer. A firm bandage should be applied to the leg to hold the dressing in place. Once the surface of the ulcer is clean and dry it should begin to heal. Ultraviolet light applied to the wound by the physiotherapist at this stage, often helps to speed up the process of healing. The patients' diet should be well balanced and nourishing. If all this fails, surgical intervention may be necessary and a skin graft will have to be performed.

Psychological support

Many of the patients nursed on rheumatology wards are suffering from chronic disabling diseases. It is therefore common for patients to have repeated hospital admissions. It is important that the nurse remembers this and tries to make their stay in hospital as pleasant and relaxed as possible, so they do not dread re-admission or put it off when it could be of benefit to them.

The aim of treatment for the chronically disabled is to allow them to lead as independent, normal and pain-free a life as possible. In order to encourage independence while in hospital it is important that the ward is suitably equipped. Bath boards, toilet raises, adapted handles are all essential on a rheumatology ward. Showers are a good idea as many people are unable to take a bath unaided. Patients themselves often make helpful suggestions about alterations and adaptations and these should be acted upon if it all possible.

Suffering from a chronic disabling disease such as rheumatoid arthritis must be very frightening and depressing for one can never be sure how much worse the disease is going to get or whether it will in fact 'burn itself out'. Whilst the patient is suffering from a 'flare-up' of the disease the constant pain and stiffness makes him very miserable. Sometimes patients begin to lose faith in their treatment and feel 'they have tried everything'. It is part of the nurse's job to encourage patients to adhere to their treatment, whilst informing the doctor of their worries. As well as this, the nurse must be aware of the inevitable worries that patients have about the future. A young mother may be worried about how she will cope with her very active children, the man of the family may be worried about his job and therefore the family's livelihood, the patient who lives on the top floor of a five-storey block of flats with no lifts may be worried about how he will manage.

The nurse can talk these problems through with the patient and also call in the help of the medical social worker, who can give practical assistance in many cases.

Patients' families should, if possible, be included in these discussions. The way in which people cope with their disablement varies tremendously and the effort they put into their treatment varies as well. The nurse must be sympathetic and understanding to all and help them to reach the peak of their ability.

In a proportion of people admitted to hospital suffering from low back pain, depression and problems of some kind are a contributory factor. These patients require sympathetic counselling as well as the physical treatments available. The nurse's attitude and encouragement can help them to be more receptive to treatment and to advice from social workers and sometimes psychiatrists.

In all these cases it is important to remember that a smiling face and sympathetic attitude can make such a difference to the confidence and morale of the patient in hospital.

Specific procedures

Specific procedures are often carried out on a rheumatology ward. These include intra-articular injections/aspiration of joints, arthroscopy, extradural injection, and radiculogram.

Intra-articular injections

A nurse on a rheumatology ward will constantly be required to prepare trolleys and assist the medical staff with intra-articular injections of steroids.

An aseptic technique is used and the puncture site is covered with a plaster until the bleeding stops. If a weight-bearing joint has been injected the patient may be confined to bed for anything up to 48 hours. There are not usually any side effects after these injections. Sometimes patients will say that they feel much better generally after an injection. This is due to the steroid which has entered the general circulation. They may also develop a flushed, red face a few hours after the injection. This is normal.

As often happens in rheumatoid arthritis, fluid collects in certain joints, especially knees, and before the steroid is injected into the joint, the fluid should be aspirated by the doctor, saved, and sent to the pathology laboratory to be cultured, to check that there is no infection, or if there is, that it can be treated with the appropriate antibiotics.

The nurse should know if both procedures are to be carried out, in order to equip the trolley correctly.

Arthroscopy

Arthroscopy is a procedure carried out on patients with painful knees to try to ascertain the cause of the pain. It is normally carried out in the operating theatre under aseptic conditions. The patient has therefore to be prepared in a gown, having signed the consent form; premedication of diazepam (Valium) 10 mg intramuscularly is given approximately one hour before the operation. Arthroscopy itself is the passing of an instrument into the knee, enabling the doctor to look into the knee and occasionally a biopsy of synovium is taken.

Nursing Care. The patient's temperature, pulse, respiration and blood pressure should be checked on his return to the ward. The affected knee is bandaged up, therefore if there is any oozing of blood, or if the patient starts complaining of severe pain, the nurse should report to the doctor. The patient sometimes has a couple of sutures in situ, which should be removed in anything up to five days.

The patient should remain in bed for 24 hours, when the bandage is removed and physiotherapy, knee and quadriceps exercises commenced. The patient is usually discharged within a few days if no gross abnormality is found and should return to out-patients at a later date, by which time the results of the biopsy should have been obtained and treatment commenced accordingly.

Extradural injection

Extradural injections (EDI) are performed regularly on some rheumatology wards and involve the injection of steroids into the extradural space using an aseptic technique. The nurse will again have to prepare the trolley and assist the medical staff with the procedure.

Afterwards the patient has to lie flat in bed until gentle mobilization is commenced on the orders of a doctor. The patient is allowed up to commode only.

Side effects again are rare; sometimes the back may be tender locally at the site of the injection. Very occasionally the patient may develop a headache following EDI; this should be reported to the doctor as it may be caused by CSF leak.

Radiculogram

The radiculogram is a radio-opaque X-ray, similar to a myelogram but only involving the lumbar spine and using a water-soluble dye. It is performed on patients with signs and symptoms of a prolapsed intervertebral disc which has not responded to medical treatment. The patient has to sit upright for six to eight hours after his return from the X-ray department and then must lie flat for at least 24 hours.

Side effects. Many patients develop a headache and they must not be moved until it has cleared. A small proportion of patients also suffer from nausea and vomiting. Once again they should continue to rest until the nausea has cleared and they should be given suitable anti-emetic and analgesic drugs as required.

14

Physiotherapy for the Rheumatic Patient

Pamela Maloney

The first need of the therapeutic team is to appreciate all the preconceived ideas the patient may have about rheumatic disease. Overcoming some of the 'old wives' tales' may be the most important hurdle to be surmounted in the beginning. For example, very many patients believe that if they stop exercising they will 'seize up' altogether. Rheumatism is a term used by the general public to embrace muscle and joint aches and pains, whether they are due to inflammatory or degenerative joint disease, capsulitis, tendinitis or muscular strains. Arthritis is understood to mean the gross destructive changes seen in people suffering from long-term rheumatoid arthritis. The general public are unwilling to accept the diagnosis 'arthritis' for the symptoms of osteoarthritis because they fear it means they will in time suffer the same gross changes they have seen in patients with rheumatic disease.

The therapeutic team is concerned with the overall care of patients and there is constant overlapping of the roles of team members; it is important that they all have an understanding of one or another's particular tasks, in order to achieve full cooperation in the treatment plan. Thus, when nurses are giving blanket baths, they are in an ideal situation to detect any increase in swelling of joints, alteration in range of movement or increase in pain. Conversely, physiotherapists can assist nurses by demonstrating how much the patient can help in

moving about the bed, without causing an increase in pain in
the affected joints. Throughout the whole treatment
programme, a constant awareness of one another's aims
and activities will create an atmosphere of confidence in
which the patient can extract the maximum benefit from the
treatment.

Arthritis is the most common condition requiring treatment
by the physiotherapist. It may be of the inflammatory kind, the
most common being rheumatoid arthritis with its associated
systemic features; the other type is degenerative joint disease,
osteoarthritis. Whatever the cause, the most disabling feature is
pain. Because of the pain there may be limitation of movement
causing disability, and subsequent loss of joint range, weakness
of muscles and loss of mobility. Anxiety and depression may
also be accompanying factors.

The patients' reaction to the pain and disability caused by
these conditions will be directly influenced by their personality
and their social and educational background. All members of
the team caring for these patients must make sure that the
patients understand the disease process, in order to participate
in the therapy. The therapy must also be acceptable within
their daily living activities. A mother with young children will
find it much more difficult to institute a programme including
regular rest periods than a person with no family commit-
ments. Patients' families must also be made aware of the need
to regulate their daily activities. A husband will find it much
easier to accept the wearing of night splints by his wife if he
understands the therapeutic need of them.

Most commonly patients will seek the advice of their general
practitioner because they can no longer accept the pain and
loss of activity caused by the disease. The aim of treatment is to
control the disease process and enable patients to live a
normal, active and comfortable life. The cardinal aims of
treatment are:

1. To reduce pain
2. To improve muscle power
3. To restore function
4. To prevent or correct deformities

Reduction of pain

Pain can be effectively relieved by rest, either by immobilizing the inflamed joint or, where there is an associated systemic reaction or a polyarthritis, by bed rest. This may be instituted at home but often it becomes necessary to admit the patient to hospital. It is quite noticeable how much the busy housewife benefits; within 48 hours of admission she will admit to feeling guilty to be occupying a hospital bed as she feels so much better. This is possibly due to the mental relief derived from no longer having to push herself to carry out the family duties despite the pain.

Degenerative joints should also be rested when they are acutely painful. It is not necessary, and indeed it is inadvisable, to rest these patients in bed as they are usually older patients and subject to the common hazards of bed rest in the elderly. Frequent rest intervals should be advised, also avoidance of stairs and carrying heavy shopping bags. Walking aids will also relieve pain.

Improvement of muscle power

During the period of bed rest, muscle tone must be maintained in all muscle groups by isometric exercises. These should be commenced as soon as the acute stage has passed. Gradual mobilization can begin as soon as the inflammation has subsided. Exercises should precede ambulation.

Restoration of function

The aim of the team is to make the patient as independent as the disease process allows by the use of exercise, hydrotherapy and splinting and by the activities of the occupational therapy department; the patient's return home can be made easier with the help of the medical social worker.

Prevention or correction of deformity

Splints are used to rest inflamed joints and give relief of pain, to prevent or correct deformity and to fix affected joints in a good position.

Resting splints

When joints are hot, painful and swollen, resting splints are worn to maintain the limb in a good position and to immobilize the affected joints.

Patients with hot, swollen joints adopt a position which gives them the greatest pain relief. The hands are held close to the chest with the fingers and wrists flexed. Painful knees are flexed, and in order to support the leg it is rested on the bed by outwardly rotating the hip. These positions can give rise to adaptive shortening of the soft tissues around the joints with resulting contractures and deformities.

If a well-fitting plaster is made the patient will obtain relief of pain because the joint is supported in a good position which allows the muscles acting on the joint to relax. Sometimes it may be necessary to aspirate the joint and inject local anaesthetic and methylprednisolone acetate before the application of the splint.

A patient may not have worn resting splints before his first admission to hospital. If they are well-fitting and give relief of pain there will be no resistance to the wearing of them. They

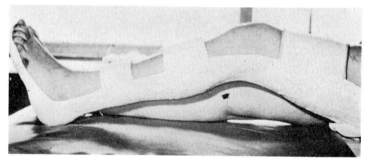

Fig. 14.1. Leg in posterior plaster of Paris slab. Immobilization is achieved by the cuffs above and below the knee.

may initially cause a disturbance of sleeping habits. Nurses, as well as physiotherapists, must encourage the patients to persevere with their splints. It is very important, for the night nurse particularly, to understand the need for such splinting. It often seems that it is far better for the patient if the splint is removed at night and the patient settled down to sleep. It is often more acceptable to splint alternate legs at night. It must be realized that splints will never be accepted if they are removed the moment the patient complains of discomfort.

Prevention of deformity

Legs. For the legs plaster back slabs are made which extend from the gluteal fold and include the foot. The foot should be at a right angle and there should be 3 degrees of flexion at the knee. These plasters must be well-fitting and smooth on the inside.

Leg plasters are made with the patient in the prone position and the feet over the end of the plinth. If, however, there is gross upper limb involvement this may be unacceptable. Plasters can be made by suspending the leg in a good position with a right angle at the ankle and 3 degrees of flexion at the knee by using conforming bandage to maintain the position. The bandage may be incorporated in the splint.

Where continuous immobilization is necessary, cuffs of plaster bandage can be applied above and below the knee and above the ankle (Fig. 14.1). This leaves the knee free for inspection. When continuous immobilization is no longer necessary, the cuffs can be removed and the plaster back slabs bandaged on at night and during day-time rest periods.

Some patients with bilateral plasters find it difficult to use a bed pan without fouling the plasters. If this is so, the plasters can be shortened enough to permit use of a bed pan without losing the immobilizing effect on the knee.

Elbow splints. Elbows can be splinted by the application of posterior plaster slabs with the elbow in 90 degrees of flexion. Since wrists and hands are also involved in the disease process and need to be included in the splints, this makes the plaster too cumbersome to be tolerated. As a rule, therefore, elbow splintage is not usually performed. Hand and wrist splints are preferable.

Hand splints. Hand splints can be made of plaster of Paris or any of the new materials available such as orthoplast. The wrist should be in a few degrees of extension and the metacarpophalangeal, proximal interphalangeal and distal interphalangeal joints should be slightly flexed to a functional position. If the hand is badly deformed, plaster bandages will give a more intimate contact. The plaster extends from just below the elbow to the fingertips. If there are nodules at the elbow the plaster must be shaped to prevent pressure on these

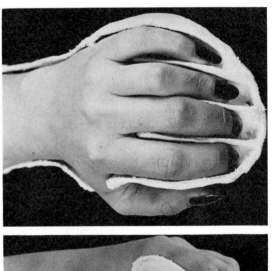

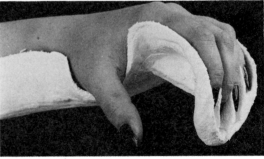

Fig. 14.2. Plaster of Paris resting hand splint. The ridges prevent crowding of the fingers.

raised areas. The plaster is made to wrap around the ulnar border of the hand and fingers to prevent ulnar deviation. Crowding of the fingertips may result, and can be overcome by adding ridges of plaster between the fingers (Fig. 14.2). The thumbs are left free unless they are acutely involved. This allows the patient to pull up the bedclothes.

Correction of deformity

Serial splinting is used to overcome a fixed deformity of a joint. These splints are worn all the time and may be complete cylinders or back slabs held on by plaster cuffs.

Serial splinting is used for fixed flexion deformity of the knees. The plasters are made with the knee in the most extended position that can be obtained without causing gross discomfort. The splints must be fixed with plaster cuffs and should be changed at weekly intervals until the best result is obtained.

Flexion deformity of the hips sometimes accompanies a fixed flexion deformity of the knees. Even if there is no fixed flexion, the hips will always be flexed while the patient is in bed. Hip flexion can be avoided by nursing the patient on a half mattress placed on top of the normal mattress, so that the feet are lower than the hips. However, a careful watch must be made to make sure the circulation is not affected by the position.

Fixed flexion of the elbows can be overcome by posterior back slabs bandaged on, with the elbow in maximum degree of extension. It is not usual to use a permanent splint on the elbow since this would needlessly prevent patients feeding themselves. Elbow splints should be worn during rest periods. Wrists are best held by a plaster cylinder, which fixes the wrists but leaves the fingers and thumbs free. The wrists should be fixed in a few degrees of extension, or if there is a fixed flexion present, in as much extension as is obtainable.

Fixation splints

It may be necessary to fix painful or unstable joints in a functional position to facilitate movement.

Knees. Unstable knees can be stabilized by the application of plaster slabs, but in providing enough rigidity this form of splint becomes too heavy to wear, and other plastic materials are used in preference. Moulded plastic cylinders can be very helpful if the other leg and arms are unaffected. Knee corsets with hinged aluminium side supports are more comfortable to wear than plaster or plastic cylinders, and allow the patient to sit easily.

Ankles. Painful ankles cause severe abnormal foot postures. The medial border collapses and the foot is turned into a valgus position. During the acute stage a walking plaster which holds the foot in a correct position may be applied. If a rocker is included in the plaster it makes a heel–toe movement possible and so improves the walking pattern. If a long-term splint is necessary a below-knee caliper can be provided but is not always accepted by the patient. Nowadays, with vacuum moulding being available, a moulded plastic back splint which includes the ankle and is worn inside the shoe and fixed by a strap around the calf just below the knee is much less conspicuous.

Wrists. Fixation splints for the wrist can provide a grip and enable walking aids to be used. They should be lightweight and washable, so that they can be used for household tasks. There are several synthetic materials on the market from which these splints can be moulded and then fixed with Velcro strips.

Neck. Patients with rheumatoid arthritis may suffer from neck pain caused by instability of the atlantoaxial joint. The instability may be due to erosion of the odontoid process or the annular ligament, causing the atlas to slip forward on the axis when the neck is flexed. Indeed, on routine flexion X-ray, patients are often found to have this instability without showing any symptoms. It is difficult to decide whether to advise the wearing of a collar or not when there are no symptoms, and the doctor will make that decision.

In severe cases the condition must be corrected by surgery but more often in the elderly a soft collar will give sufficient support. If the wearing of a soft collar does not provide enough support, a more rigid collar can be made of plasterzote. This is best if moulded to each individual, and care must be taken that the fixation is as easy as possible for the patient with affected arms.

When pain is not relieved by means of a rigid collar and it is necessary to restrict rotation of the neck, a larger collar is necessary. This supports the neck at the occiput and the chin, and is held in place by a back and breast plate, supported on the shoulders. The chin piece must be removable for eating.

Muscle and joint management

During the period of bed rest the patient should be instructed in a programme of exercises to maintain joint range and muscle tone for all unaffected limbs. This is an important time in the relationship between physiotherapist and patient and will directly affect the patient's attitude to the treatment programme. Time must be taken to explain the reasons for the exercises and the need to continue the exercises at home.

Passive movement of affected joints is contraindicated because the increasing pain causes muscle spasm but isometric exercises for muscle groups of affected joints can be commenced when they do not give rise to pain.

For patients with affected knee joints, treatment starts with isometric exercises for the quadriceps. These are followed by flexion exercises and straight leg raising, commenced slowly and gradually increased in number. Any increase in pain and swelling should be noted and the number of exercises reduced until the inflammation has settled.

As these exercises become easier, straight leg raising can be advanced by the addition of 1–2 kg weights to the ankle. The final degrees of extension can best be obtained by supporting the knee on a small padded block and practising knee extension exercises. When a patient has learnt a programme of exercises and performs them correctly, daily exercise periods can be unsupervised. This is not possible if the patient is under the bedclothes or there is a cradle in the bed. With the cooperation of the nursing staff it is preferable to have patients lying on top of the bed with a light cover over their legs for warmth. This can be pushed aside for the exercise period and pulled over again on completion of activity. Continental quilts are an ideal form of bed covering for rheumatoid patients. They are so light that even those most severely affected in hands and wrists can cope with them.

As the inflammation subsides and the muscle strength improves, weight-bearing is commenced. The patient can stand out of bed and practise standing and sitting, progressing to walking increasing distances. Patients with joint disease must continue the programmes at home. Quadriceps drill should become a way of life; ankle, hand, elbow and shoulder exercises a daily routine. Patients are more likely to follow a routine if the exercises can be carried out without interfering with family life. Quadriceps drill can be easily carried out while watching television and a couple of bags of sugar in a stocking can be used for added weight. Exercises for other affected joints can be prescribed in a similar manner.

Patients with lower limb involvement spend most of their day sitting in a chair and therefore must be persuaded to spend at least one hour during the day either in a prone position or if this is too uncomfortable, lying flat on the bed. Gluteal contractions must be carried out if it is not possible to perform extension exercises for the hips. If nurses are aware of this need they will cooperate by ensuring that their patients are correctly positioned for these rest periods.

For patients with affected hands and wrists, shoulders and elbows must be exercised. These joints are used only in order to move the functioning part of the upper limb, i.e. the hand, to the appropriate position for performing different activities. If pain precludes the use of the hands, it follows that elbows and shoulders are little used. Shoulders must be exercised through a full range of movement, with emphasis on rotation and extension. If standing can only be achieved by pushing up on the arms of a chair, then there must be extension and rotation at the shoulder joint. The triceps must be exercised in order to assist the same activity.

Ability to use the hands is essential for independence, and a good grip must be maintained. Flexion and extension of the fingers must be pushed to the fullest range, particularly at the carpometacarpal joints. Providing there is no acute inflammation present, passive movements to the small joints of the fingers may be necessary. In addition, exercises to overcome ulnar deviation must be performed, such as placing the hands on a flat surface and taking each finger towards the mid line. Flexion and extension of the wrist will be made easier by fixing the forearm with the other hand if this is possible.

Tension of the neck and shoulders often causes great discomfort when patients are on bed rest and wearing splints. Exercises for the muscles of the shoulder girdle, shoulder shrugging and shoulder retraction, will help to ease the tightness in this area. Neck exercises can be given, providing there is no instability at the atlantoaxial joint.

Pain in any of the joints of the lower limb will affect walking and this will affect the posture of the patient and throw a strain on the back. Flexion deformity of the hips and knees will cause a lumbar lordosis and probably a considerable amount of backache. Trunk exercises must be given to maintain and improve the abdominal muscles and help to improve posture.

Continuing out-patient treatment for a patient with severe joint disease is not necessary if the patient understands the need for home exercises, and maintains a regular exercise routine. The journey to and from the hospital often undoes any good the treatment may give. The hospital visits do fulfil a social function for the patient who lives alone but with the help of the social worker it is better to find a club nearer home than to make long journeys to hospital and use scarce resources.

Hydrotherapy

Hydrotherapy is a useful form of treatment for patients with joint disease and is an ideal way of initiating activity in a rheumatoid patient who has just undergone a period of rest.

The warmth of the water (about 36°C) helps to relieve pain and induces relaxation of the muscles. This will allow a greater range of movement in the affected joints. The warmth of the water will also increase the blood supply to the skin and muscles, improving their condition and improving muscle contraction.

The pool area must be kept warm as disabled patients are slow-moving and will take longer to dry and dress after treatment. After treatment patients should rest for some time in the physiotherapy department before being returned to the wards as in so many departments this means going into the open and being exposed to the elements.

Patients should shower after pool treatment to reduce the effects of skin irritation by the chlorine in the water or a variation in the pH factor (if pH factor falls below 7.2–7.8, skin irritation may occur). Patients with rheumatoid arthritis often have thin skin and if they scratch because of a skin irritation it is very easy to break the surface of the skin.

The buoyancy of the water supports the limbs and allows exercises to be performed with far less effort than on land. The patient can be put in a free floating position with the aid of floats. Exercises for all the limbs can be given in this position with the limbs supported by the water. Trunk exercises can also be given in this position with the physiotherapist fixing the shoulders and the patient moving the trunk. Helped by the buoyancy of the water, the patient who has difficulty in standing and walking can practise changing from sitting on a bench in the water to standing and walking before attempting these activities on land.

Patients with joint disease of the lower limbs spend a long time in the sitting position. Floating will therefore stretch the anterior capsule of the hip joints. By altering the starting positions all the muscles around the hip joints can be exercised, first with buoyancy assistance and then against the resistance of the water. This will improve not only the tone of the muscles but also the joint range. The quadriceps can also be exercised in this way and the resistance increased by the use of floats.

The upper limbs can be exercised by sitting the patient on a bench with the arms floating on the surface of the water or with the patient in a free floating position. The length of the weight arm can be increased by the use of 'ping-pong bats' of light wood.

Care must be taken when transferring patients from the changing room to the pool. If the patient is heavy and immobile a hoist should be used with one therapist attending to the patient as he/she is lifted off the chair or stretcher, and another therapist waiting in the pool to receive the patient.

Walking on wet floors is a hazard for anyone, but more so for patients with stiff and weak limbs. They should be escorted to and fro until they have acquired the habit of walking with extra care. The floor should be covered with studded tiles that drain away the spilled water. In the later stages of mobilization, exercises on dry land are necessary to obtain the final degrees of movement.

Hydrotherapy is a form of treatment that most patients enjoy and participate in with enthusiasm. They should be encouraged to use their own swim-suits if they have them or if the department provides them, let them be as attractive as possible. Those patients with a great fear of water should never be made to undergo hydrotherapy as it causes great anxiety and the benefits of the treatment will be lost.

Heat and ice treatments

Heat or ice may be used to reduce joint swelling and muscle spasm during an acute flare-up of an affected joint and may continue to be used prior to exercise. The choice of heat or ice therapy is made according to the best effect on the individual patient.

Heat

The large joints are best treated by short-wave therapy using the through-and-through method or the coil. Infra-red lamps can also be used to heat these joints and are particularly useful when the cervical spine and shoulders are subject to pain and spasm. An increasingly popular form of applying heat to the neck, shoulders and the back is the electric heat pad. Great comfort is derived from lying on these pads and there is the added advantage that these appliances can be used in the ward and in the home. Hot water bottles have a limited use. Paraffin wax baths, temperature 38°C, are probably best for the hands, particularly following hand surgery. The hands are sweaty and slightly greasy after the wax treatment which has a softening effect on the skin. Patients can then exercise without the sudden cracking of the hard skin around the incision, making them afraid the wound will break down. Paraffin wax treatment in the home necessitates the use of a double saucepan and a wax thermometer and is an unnecessary fire hazard. A simple alternative is to wear loose household gloves and immerse the hands in hot water.

Ice

Ice may be the treatment of choice for some patients, particularly those who complain of an increase in pain when they get warm in bed. Ice packs can be used for the large joints. These are made of crushed ice in plastic bags which can then be wrapped in a towel and applied to the affected joints. Closer contact can be made by using towels wrung out in iced water. This may be the best method of covering a larger area of the knee and shoulder but has the possible disadvantage of wetting the patient's clothes.

Hands can be treated by immersion in a bowl of water and crushed ice. The hands are kept in the ice until they start aching and then brought out and exercised, continuing in this way for about five minutes. It is also possible for the patient to administer ice therapy in the home. There are on the market special thermal packs for use in picnic hampers which can be used many times as an ice pack.

Heat and ice treatments can be given by the patients in their own homes provided they first appreciate that the treatments not only help to relieve pain but also improve exercise performance. It is important that the patient realizes the function of heat in particular. It is very comforting to have warmth applied to painful joints. However, if patients then exercise without adequate understanding they are likely to think that heat makes them better because it is a passive form of treatment and there is relief of pain, and that exercise makes them worse because there is an increase in pain. In consequence they will be inclined to omit the exercises.

Ultrasound

Ultrasound is used mainly in the treatment of local soft tissue inflammation, for example, plantar fasciitis, bursitis or tendonitis. Ultrasonics can also be used for localized treatment of leg ulcers.

Mobility

Being able to walk does not make a patient independent if he is unable to walk unaided and this is the most difficult activity to achieve, particularly when there is upper limb involvement. Chair height is crucial. Frequently the height of the chair which facilitates easy standing means the chair is too high to sit on and when sitting, the feet are not supported. Arms of chairs are often too far behind the patient when he has moved his weight forward and can no longer use his arms to push up. The best chairs are adjustable in height and have much longer arms than is usual. Ejector chairs are available but their use meets with understandable resistance because patients are afraid of them.

Having manoeuvred themselves into an upright position, patients cannot walk far if their feet are very painful. Comfortable shoes are difficult to obtain as the disease distorts the foot contours so as to make most shoes obtainable on the general market unsuitable. Space shoes and the most recent plasterzote shoes can be moulded to fit misshapen feet and provide a greater degree of comfort and stability. Insoles can be made of plasterzote which is moulded to the individual foot. Medical support can be added to overcome the collapse of the long arch and metatarsal heads. Sponge pads under the heel can ease the discomfort of a plantar fasciitis.

Walking aids

Walking aids are generally provided by the physiotherapist.

They are used when weight relief is required for the lower limbs, and for patients who are unsteady on their feet and require some form of aid to remedy this. Understanding their correct use and function will enable the nursing staff to encourage independence without anxiety.

The choice of aid will be directly related to the degree of involvement of the upper limbs in the disease process. Light-weight elbow crutches of adjustable length can be used by most people with minimum involvement of upper limbs. They should also have adjustable arm supports in order to avoid pressure on painful nodules at the elbow. The crutch height should be adjusted to suit each patient when standing and the elbow should be in a few degrees of flexion. For those patients with upper limb involvement gutter crutches can be used. Even they may need to be modified to fit gross deformities of wrist or fingers. For patients with poor balance a walking frame will give greater confidence. It may be necessary when hands and wrists are severely involved to modify these frames, i.e. adding gutter supports, and when the weight is a problem using the frames with wheels on the leading legs.

It is often very difficult to persuade patients to use walking aids and often it is some time before they can be persuaded to use a walking stick. It may be necessary to modify the handles to fit the distorted hand. There are on the market some sticks with moulded left and right hands. It is the physiotherapist's task to find the best means of helping each individual patient. If the aids provided make it easier for the patient to move about, he will continue to use them. The aim is to restore his independence; however these walking aids, since they involve the use of the hands, tend to restrict other self-help activities in the home. Trolleys of the correct height can help overcome this problem by providing a means of weight relief and a carrying surface for movement about the house.

The chair-bound patient

When the joint changes are so great as to make it impossible for patients to walk, their degree of independence will be directly related to their upper limb involvement. If the patient has strong upper limbs he can maintain a high degree of independence in a wheelchair; he can transfer from bed to chair and chair to commode and perform many household tasks as well as propelling himself about the house. He will also be able to get out of the house.

Patients with upper limb involvement can also be surprisingly independent if they have enough strength to stand and transfer from bed to chair, etc. It is surprising how independent some patients with gross changes in both arms and legs are, even managing to live alone with the support of the social services.

Boredom is one of the greatest disadvantages of the chair-bound patient and often leads to heavy smoking and overeating with the consequent hazards of such overindulgence. The dietitian can provide assistance by advising a suitable varied and interesting menu. Attendance at day centres can make life more interesting for these patients by enlarging their social contacts and intellectual pursuits.

Some common conditions

Neck pain

Degenerative joint disease of the apophyseal joints of the cervical spine can give rise to severe neck pain with referred pain if there is nerve root compression. Any pain in the neck will cause a severe protective spasm of the neck muscles with reduction of neck movements and possible torticollis.

Heat, by means of an electric heat pad, will help to reduce the muscle spasm and may be necessary before the neck can be examined. Passive and active neck movements should be measured and the pain distribution recorded before treatment is commenced.

Traction can give some relief of pain. Massage is a useful means of aiding muscle relaxation and can lead into manipulative techniques by reassuring the patient that handling of the head and neck need not necessarily be painful.

Manipulation is a skill which should be practised by experienced people who have been adequately trained in the techniques.

Low back pain

As in the cervical spine degenerative changes in the apophyseal joints of the lumbar spine can give rise to low back pain and pressure of the nerve roots will give rise to pain in the distribution areas. The pain will be accompanied by muscle spasm and changes of posture in order to adopt the most comfortable position.

Treatment will again be heat, lumbar traction and manipulation and the previous precaution should be observed. Manipulations of the lumbar spine require far more force and should be practised by experienced physiotherapists with special training in these techniques.

Lumbar disc lesions

It is often necessary for patients to be admitted for a period of bed rest when pressure from a prolapsed disc causes nerve root compression. The aim of treatment is to immobilize the lumbar spine to allow resolution of the localized inflammation. Traction will help to immobilize the spine and give relief of pain. In some centres epidural injections of anti-inflammatory drugs (hydrocortisone) are used to speed up the resolution of inflammation.

If the prolapse is small it may be possible to proceed to early mobilization, correction of posture and exercises to improve the tone of the muscles supporting the spine. The abdominal musculature is very important and is often very slack in a patient with poor posture. Isometric exercises can be commenced for the abdominal muscles while the patient is on bed rest.

It may be necessary to apply a plaster cast when the patient begins to mobilize or a corset may be recommended. If it is necessary to immobilize the spine in this way, the patient should have exercises to mobilize the spine when the cast or corset is discarded. Some patients once wrapped up in a corset

are loath to part with it and can be found years later still
wearing a corset with a stiff lumbar spine and flabby musculature.

If the prolapse is large, surgical intervention may be
necessary to relieve nerve root pressure. Following surgery
passive straight leg raising should be commenced on the first
day, and trunk movement and spinal extension exercises
commenced when advised by the surgeon. These exercises
reduce the possibility of scar tissue forming round the nerve
root and causing further pain. Any weakness of muscles caused
by the nerve root pressure must also be treated by exercise.

Ankylosing spondylitis

Ankylosing spondylitis is a chronic inflammatory disease
involving apophyseal joints, cartilaginous joints of the spine
and the sacroiliac joints. Other peripheral joints may be
involved. It is a painful condition and the patient complains of
backache and stiffness. The stiffness is much worse in the
morning. There may be loss of cervical and lumbar lordotic
curves.

Patients with ankylosing spondylitis may be admitted to
hospital for medical treatment. During their stay it is advisable
to institute an intensive programme of exercises and to explain
the need for exercises to be carried out every day. Providing
the drugs prescribed give sufficient relief of pain, spinal and
chest mobility exercises may be taught. These exercises should
be reasonably simple so that they can be remembered and
continued at home.

Advice should be given to improve posture. A firm mattress
with one pillow should be used and periods of prone lying will
help to prevent or correct deformity. It is also necessary to give
advice on sitting and standing. Desk and chair should be at
the correct height to prevent stooping at work.

Soft tissue conditions

Patients admitted to hospital for the treatment of arthritis may
also present with other painful areas, the most common being

the shoulder. Careful examination must be carried out to ascertain the cause of the pain, whether it is referred from the neck or due to inflammation of the joint capsule. Joint range should be recorded. Capsulitis may well lead to 'frozen shoulder' if the arm is kept immobile.

Ice packs applied to the muscles of the shoulder girdle will relieve pain and assisted exercises should start gently and be within the limits of pain. The exercises can be progressed to free active and then resisted exercises as the condition improves. For the frozen shoulder Maitlands Manipulations can be used with good effect. As the joint range increases, exercise can be introduced. Pool therapy is also beneficial for shoulder pain.

The patient with a painful shoulder is constantly guarding against movement and keeps the arm held closely to the side. If it is necessary for the patient to be lifted by the nursing staff they must be made aware of this condition and take appropriate action to avoid causing further pain. Shoulder exercises should always be related to household tasks in order that patients learn what they can do at home. It sometimes happens that patients attending for out-patient treatment three times a week are doing nothing at home because of their 'bad shoulder'.

Assessment of results

The effectiveness of treatment cannot be assessed unless there is careful and accurate measurement of joint range, muscle strength, etc. before treatment is commenced. Included in this assessment should be a record of the degree of independence and social activities of the patient.

Knowledge of the home environment is necessary as is the help available to the patient on return home. The patient should also be given the opportunity to say what he regards as his greatest handicap. Patients do not always give the same priority to activity as do the therapeutic staff. It has been known for a patient to feel very disgruntled when, having had his disease treated and clinical and laboratory tests having shown a return to normality, he is still suffering from the original disability. It is particularly important to learn from the patient how he has overcome his difficulties himself. In particular, much can be learned from the efforts of the severely handicapped patient in acquiring independence.

15

Occupational Therapy, Rehabilitation and Resettlement

Janet Douglas

How does occupational therapy help the patient with rheumatoid arthritis? Mainly it helps by showing him how to perform those simple daily tasks that the able-bodied take for granted, such as how to get his tablets out of the bottle and how to comb his hair if he cannot touch the back of his head. This chapter outlines the main ways in which occupational therapy can benefit these patients. Basic methods of treatment are described, with details of where to obtain further information. When treating patients with rheumatoid arthritis, occupational therapists should aim to give the patients encouragement and hope whilst being realistic about their disability. Many newly diagnosed patients are very scared and worried about the prospect of being disabled and deformed, and fear rejection by their families because they may become a burden to them. Rheumatoid arthritis can be a very crippling disease but in such cases the occupational therapist can help alleviate the difficulties experienced by teaching the patient how to cope with his disability. This needs a positive and understanding approach.

Aims of treatment

In the treatment of patients with rheumatoid arthritis the occupational therapist has five main aims:

1. To prevent deformity
2. To improve the patient's physical condition
3. To help the patient reach his maximum level of independence
4. To aid the patient's emotional adjustment to his disability
5. To resettle the patient into the community

It is important that these five aims be remembered during all stages of treatment, because it is essential to treat the patient as a whole person and not merely to treat his disability.

Whether working in hospital or in the community the occupational therapist is a member of the rehabilitation team. Good communication between all members of the team is vital if an effective treatment programme is to be planned and carried out. The occupational therapist must therefore inform the team, including its most important member, the patient, of the aims of treatment and how they can fulfil the patient's specific needs. It is essential for the therapist to gain the patient's confidence and cooperation from the start. If this is not done there is no point in continuing treatment as it will not be successful.

Assessment

When the patient is first referred the occupational therapist will carry out an assessment. This should be an assessment of the whole patient, including his physical condition, functional ability and emotional adjustment to his disability.

Physical assessment

The range and power of movement of each joint should be measured and recorded. This is sometimes difficult and uncomfortable for the patient, and in such cases a functional assessment may be more beneficial and realistic. For example, this may involve getting the patient to pick up various objects which requires the use of different types of grip, and by reaching to touch different parts of the body. The assessment should be carried out bilaterally to allow comparison. Regular reassessments should be done. The time between these will depend on the patient's condition. When the disease is active reassessment should be carried out more frequently than when the patient is having a remission.

Activities of daily living assessment

When assessing a patient's ability to manage activities of daily living (ADL) the therapist should adopt a positive attitude by seeing what the patient can do, not what he cannot do. There are no standardized assessment forms but most occupational therapy departments will have their own. Providing that these cover all aspects of the patient's life and that the method of recording the information so obtained is easy to understand, then they should be satisfactory.

To carry out a proper assessment the therapist must first find out about the patient's home situation which will involve asking about the type of accommodation, the facilities both in the home and locally, and the help provided either by family and friends or by the local social services department or voluntary organizations. The therapist must also find out whether or not the patient works or if he has any deadlines to meet such as being dressed when the transport arrives to take him to a day-centre. These factors should be taken into account when prescribing aids after the full ADL assessment has been carried out as additional aids may be needed if the patient has a time-limit to work to.

When carrying out an ADL assessment it is important that the patient is actually seen doing the activity. Often busy therapists will just ask questions and the patient may have an unrealistic opinion of what he is able to do. The assessment should cover everything a patient is likely to do including general mobility, personal care, household activities, gardening and recreation.

It is generally best for the assessment to be divided into three or four sections to be done at consecutive attendances. Most patients, especially the severely disabled, will find a full assessment tiring and distressing, especially if they are unable to perform a number of tasks when asked. Failure is not good for the patient or for the rapport the therapist has hopefully built up. Therefore a shorter assessment of the most important activities for the patient should be carried out first and the others done later.

Work assessment

Patients who are working will need to be assessed to see if they can return to their previous employment. This will involve the therapist finding out as much as possible about the patient's type of work, the mode of transport to work and the physical lay-out and facilities of the work-place itself. The occupational therapist should try to simulate the patient's work situation. It is necessary to assess whether the patient can carry out his former job and if so whether he is able to do it full-time or only part-time. Speed and efficiency should also be tested.

If the patient is unable to return to his former employment he will need to be assessed in other work situations to see if it is feasible to try to find him alternative employment or to arrange retraining for a new occupation. A work assessment should be carried out before the occupational therapist or social worker contacts the Disablement Resettlement Officer (DRO) to ask for help to find employment for the patient.

Assessment is a waste of time if the findings are merely recorded in the patient's notes. The occupational therapist should use the findings from all the assessments to plan or replan the treatment programme.

TREATMENT

Treatment falls into four categories:

1. Preventive treatment
2. Remedial treatment
3. Management of the disability
4. Assisting the patient's emotional adjustment to his physical condition

Preventive treatment

Preventive treatment is carried out by the provision of splints and by teaching the patient the principles of joint protection. Splinting was discussed in Chapter 14 (see p. 112). Joint protection is best explained to the patient by the use of photographs.

Deformities may be prevented by using the principles of joint protection if the patient is referred to the occupational therapist soon after the condition is diagnosed. At this time the patient is usually very anxious about the prospect of becoming deformed and will follow the therapist's advice on how to take care of his joints. This advice is also helpful for patients in whom the disease has progressed, but the results are generally less successful. The basic principles are:

1. Avoid straining the joints.
2. Avoid activities which encourage typical deformities.
3. Use labour-saving equipment for work activities whenever possible.
4. Redesign work areas to avoid unnecessary bending, stretching and walking.
5. Rest joints before they become painful.
6. Sit rather than stand.
7. Do not keep in one position for too long.
8. Make sure an activity is really necessary before starting.
9. Accept help but do not become inactive and dependent.
10. Try not to be a perfectionist.

The occupational therapist should find out, preferably at first hand, about the activities the patient performs during the day whether he is at home or at work. She can then teach him to incorporate the above principles into his daily life.

The main deformities that joint protection principles can help avoid are ulnar deviation, subluxation of the metacarpophalangeal joints, flexion of the knees, flexion and adduction of the hips and plantar flexion of the ankle. To avoid ulnar deviation the strain of doing an activity should be reduced either by using a long lever or by using more than one joint, such as carrying a pile of plates by supporting them underneath with the palms and fingers of both hands held flat. Subluxation of the metacarpophalangeal joints can be avoided to a certain extent by not using the pincer grip. This will entail padding thin handles and pens and avoiding activities such as knitting which require the pincer grip. Deformities of the lower limbs are often caused by overstraining the joints. The patient should be encouraged to sit with his feet supported and knees straight on a correct height chair with a straight high back so that the head and neck are also supported. Adduction of the hips is encouraged if the patient sits with his legs or ankles crossed. This position should therefore be avoided.

Space does not permit more than this brief description of joint protection. The subject is, however, well covered by Merete Brattström in her book *Principles of Joint Protection in Chronic Rheumatic Disease**.

Remedial treatment

The patient's physical condition can be improved by using therapeutic activities to encourage and increase movement by strengthening muscles and mobilizing joints while discouraging postures typical of rheumatoid arthritis.

Once the patient has been assessed, activities should be chosen that will give the required movement. The activities should be upgraded or changed as the patient's condition

* See Appendix 1 for details of publications mentioned in this chapter.

varies. Although only one particular joint may need specific treatment attention should be paid to the whole body. Good posture should be encouraged at all times. The patient should be able to change position frequently to avoid stiffness in the joints not being exercised. Activities should be bilateral, repetitive and rhythmical. The patient should be told to rest if pain occurs except when being treated after surgery when a limited amount of pain may have to be endured.

The choice of therapeutic activity will be limited by the size and type of the department and by the patient's interests. The activity should be realistic and, if necessary and possible, prevocational. Woodwork, clerical work and household activities are all realistic and can be done in most departments. Remedial games can provide useful movements while encouraging interaction among patients. They should, however, form only part of the patient's treatment programme.

Many occupational therapists avoid using crafts. Some crafts, however, can be very therapeutic as they demand a wide variety of movements. The patient, however, must understand why he is doing the activity. Weaving, basketry and printing are activities which provide numerous movements that can be graded. Sewing on a treadle machine or doing fretwork on a treadle or bicycle fretsaw provides non-weight bearing exercise which improves the physical condition of the lower limbs while the patient makes something useful.

Weaving and printing can be adapted by using slings and pulleys to provide movements such as knee extension. These should only be used as a last resort as no patient likes to be 'strung up' and if their movements are restricted it may cause stiffness in other joints. A good therapist should be ingenious enough to obtain a required movement by choice of activity rather than by using adaptations. Some patients, however, will benefit if their limbs are suspended in slings to relieve pressure and pain. This is therapeutic provided the limb is in a good position. The O.B. Help Arm is ideal for alleviating pain in the shoulder while allowing the patient to carry out an activity such as weaving which will help to increase the range of movement in that joint.

Treatments should be carried out fairly frequently for short periods with intervals for rest. In-patients should have two half-hour treatment sessions per day if possible. This does, however, depend on their condition and amount of pain. Ideally treatments should be given after physiotherapy, especially if the patient is having wax or pool treatment as there is often an increased range of movement when the joints are warm and have been exercised by the physiotherapist. Some patients may benefit from warming their hands in warm water or from doing an activity or remedial game in a hot box before starting their main treatment programme. Loosening-up exercises such as a short keep-fit session or a few minutes working with remedial putty may be useful if the patient cannot be seen immediately after physiotherapy. Remedial putty should be avoided if the patient's hands are very deformed as it tends to stick round bent fingers which is obviously very frustrating and uncomfortable.

The patient should then continue his treatment by performing the selected activity. The purpose and method should be explained to the patient and if necessary re-explained until he understands. It is important to make sure that the patient performs the activity in the correct way and does not cheat or use an alternative method that will not give the required movement. The therapist should check this at the start of each treatment session even if the patient is carrying on where he left off. This is because the patient's condition may alter from day to day, due to such things as weather, emotional upset or simply a bad night's sleep.

Some patients benefit from being treated in a group as this provides encouragement and competition from others. It may also help to distract them from thinking about their own disability all the time and to consider others.

Management of the disability

Most patients suffering from rheumatoid arthritis will have some form of disability whether it is minimal morning stiffness or severe deformity causing dependence on other people. The

ADL assessment will show the areas where a patient needs help and advice to become more independent. When a patient has difficulty performing an everyday activity he can usually be taught an alternative technique or be supplied with an aid to help him overcome the difficulty. There are many aids and alternative techniques which can help a patient with rheumatoid arthritis to be more independent. Suppliers of aids are listed in Appendix 2, and each supplier usually provides a catalogue and price list. Therapists should write to or visit the firms or their nearest aids centre to see and evaluate what they have to offer. The Disabled Living Foundation provides information sheets on aids and their suppliers. The National Fund for Research into Crippling Diseases publishes the ten booklets in the series *Equipment for the Disabled*. Titles include Home Management, Personal Care, and Communication. The Consumers Association publishes a book called *Coping with Disablement* by Peggy Jay, which gives advice to all types of disabled person.

The provision of aids should be avoided as much as possible as they tend to be expensive and often patients do not use them when they are at home. Under the 1970 Chronically Sick and Disabled Persons Act it became the responsibility of local authorities to provide help for the disabled living in their locality. This means that many local authorities pay for the aids supplied by the hospital occupational therapist. Some authorities supply aids on loan and expect them to be returned when they are no longer needed. As there are numerous aids on the market careful consideration should be given when supplying the aid. The occupational therapist should be sure it is really necessary, that the patient understands how to use it and that there is not a cheaper version that is just as effective. Aids should only be provided permanently after a home visit has been carried out. If a patient needs a specific aid made in the department the designer should observe the basic rules of using larger handles, longer levers, lightweight materials and angled handles.

The following section discusses the work of the occupational therapist in helping patients to overcome some of the common difficulties encountered in the areas of general mobility, transferring, personal care, household activities and gardening.

General mobility

Many patients will experience difficulty in walking and getting around. The physiotherapist usually prescribes walking aids but the occupational therapist becomes involved when dealing with the mobility problems of the severely handicapped. A wheelchair may be needed for this type of patient. Although the request form is signed by the patient's doctor, it is often the role of the therapist to make the assessment and order the most suitable chair. A number of different chairs can be ordered either from the Artificial Limb and Appliance Centre (ALAC) or from one of the many commercial firms that make wheelchairs. A wheelchair ordered from ALAC is only loaned to the patient and must be returned when it is no longer needed. Chairs bought from commercial firms are expensive but they are generally more aesthetic. Before ordering a chair, the therapist should make a home visit to ensure that doorways and turning circles are big enough for the patient to manoeuvre the chair around the home. A ramp may be needed if there are steps up to the front door. When the wheelchair is delivered it is essential for the therapist to check that it functions properly and that the patient can manoeuvre it and operate the brakes.

Stairs may present a problem to the ambulant, if each stair is too high. This can be overcome by using a half step on each stair or by the patient taking a portable half step with him. For the severely disabled and wheelchair-bound patients it may be possible to have a stair lift fitted. There are many different types available and advice can be obtained from the manufacturers. Some local authorities will pay for the lift and its installation but as this is quite expensive the request has to go to various committees before it is agreed and this often causes long delays.

Getting around outside the home is very hard for the disabled, especially if they want to use public transport. Bus steps are very high and patients may have to rely on the help of others to get onto the bus. Getting into trains is just as difficult. Trains have the added difficulty of having doors to open. There is a case of a patient who always has to make sure that there are people in the carriage he is travelling in because he cannot open the door from the inside. British Rail have been approached about this and have given the New Cross Hospital occupational therapy department a door lock so that an aid can be developed to overcome the problem. A train is the only mode of public transport suitable for a patient in a wheelchair. However, the patient probably has to travel in the guard's van if he is unable to get out of his wheelchair.

Some patients prefer to travel by car. If the patient is going to drive, special adaptations may be needed so that he can handle the car safely. Advice on this can be obtained from the British School of Motoring Disability Training Centre*. Getting in and out of cars can be difficult because the seats are so low. It is usually best for the disabled passenger to sit in the front seat.

Transferring

Sitting down and standing up often pose problems for the patient with stiff, painful joints which give a limited range of movement. Transferring is easier if the seat is at the right height and is firm; this may be achieved by raising the chair on blocks and placing a board under the cushion. The same principles apply to beds. Heavy bedclothes make turning over in bed difficult. Bedclothes should be light but warm, and a continental quilt or an electric blanket may be the solution.

Patients should be encouraged to sit in a chair with their knees straight and their ankles at right angles. To do this they may need a leg rest and footstool such as the one made by SML†. Ejector seats may help the patient to get up from a chair. The patient, however, may be reluctant to use one of these because he has little control over it. Because of this a

---

* See Appendix 3 for addresses of societies and clubs.
† See Appendix 2 for sources of information, and suppliers of aids.

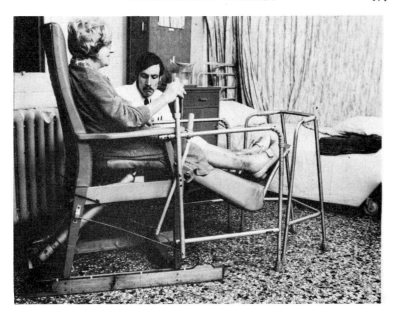

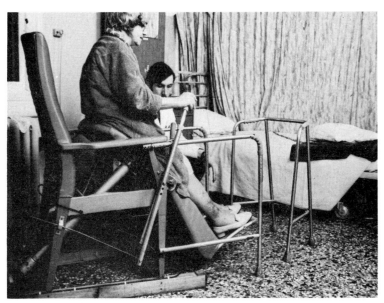

Fig. 15.1. The New Cross Hospital hydraulically operated chair. (above) Patient in sitting position prior to raising herself by operating lever. (below) Patient raised to upright position ready for walking away.

hydraulically operated self-rise chair has been made for a patient at New Cross Hospital (Fig. 15.1) and the marketing of it is being considered by the Self-Lift Chair Company. The chair allows the patient to have complete control over raising and lowering the seat. The movement can be as fast or as slow as the patient wants and allows for somebody who is unsteady on standing to get up very gradually.

The patient with rheumatoid arthritis may also have difficulties transferring in the bathroom. Showers are easier to get into than a bath but not all patients like showers. If a patient wants a shower and cannot stand for long periods he could sit on an ordinary plastic garden chair. Aids, such as a rail, bath board, bath seat and non-slip mat, may make it possible for a patient to get into the bath on his own. If possible the occupational therapist should see the patient bathing, as transferring is harder when one is wet. Some patients will need a hoist to get into the bath. An excellent one is the Auto-Lift supplied by Homecraft which allows the patient to remain sitting on the seat of the hoist while bathing. A patient may not be able to get on or off the lavatory because it is too low. A raised toilet seat and either a free standing toilet frame or a grab rail fixed to the wall may make transferring easier.

Personal care

The difficulties patients with rheumatoid arthritis experience in personal care activities are usually caused by limitation of grip and reach. It may be possible to teach the patient how to get into the bath using aids but once in he may not be able to put the plug in, turn the taps on or hold a flannel. Aids may solve these problems or it may be necessary to arrange for a District Nurse or Bathing Attendant to visit the patient when he is at home to help him to bathe. Sometimes it may be difficult to grip a towel, in which case the patient may be able to dry himself by putting on a towelling dressing gown to soak up the excess water.

Although an electric razor is the easiest type of razor to use, many patients prefer a wet shave. Cut-throat and safety razors can be adapted by lengthening and padding the handles. If the patient finds it painful to hold his hand up to his face it may help him to have a shelf put up in the bathroom to support his elbow.

Using the lavatory can be difficult due to the patient having to manage his clothing. A man may find this easier to cope with if he wears braces. A female patient may like to tuck the hems of her skirt and petticoat into a belt or piece of elastic round her waist so that she does not have to hold these up while pulling down her pants and tights. If a mirror is put in the toilet it helps the patient to make sure his clothing is properly adjusted before leaving the room.

Most dressing problems are also caused by the patient's restricted movements and weak or poor grip. Aids such as a dressing stick, 'Helping Hand' stocking dresser, and long-handled shoehorn may help the patient to be independent or his 'dressing technique' may need to be altered. It is generally easier if dressing is done sitting down. If the patient has weak arms it may help him to rest his elbows on a table while putting garments over his head. Reaching his feet may be made easier by sitting on a chair and putting his foot back and up at the side of the chair. Further information about dressing problems can be obtained from the National Fund for Research into Crippling Diseases booklet 'Clothing and Dressing for Adults' in the series *Equipment for the Disabled*. The Disabled Living Foundation has an adviser on clothing and produces booklets called *Clothes Sense for Handicapped Adults of All Ages* and *How to Adapt Existing Clothing for the Disabled*.

Patients with rheumatoid arthritis should be encouraged to look well groomed. Often people are put off approaching the disabled because they look dirty or untidy. Grooming is not easy for somebody who has deformities and is in pain. Combing the hair is difficult if there is restricted movement in the upper limbs. A long-handled comb that is angled helps the patient to reach the back of his head. Applying make-up may be painful as the hand has to be held up to the face for a long while. This can be eased by resting the elbow either on the table or on a shelf beside a mirror. A patient may neglect his nails because he cannot manicure them with the usual tools.

Cleaning the nails is made easier by fixing a nail brush to the basin by the use of suction cups and then rubbing the nails up and down the bristles. A nail file is easier to hold if it is fitted into a piece of dowel.

One of the most frustrating tasks for a patient is feeding himself. This may be difficult because he cannot hold and use the cutlery or because he cannot reach his mouth due to ulnar deviation of the wrist and restricted movements in the elbows and shoulders. Lightweight cutlery with enlarged handles or the cutlery in the Manoy range is easier to grip than standard cutlery (Fig. 15.2). The handles of the patient's own cutlery can be enlarged by using rubbazote or splinting material such as polyform. Forks and spoons can be bent to the correct angle to enable the patient to reach his mouth. Holding a cup with a conventional handle may be difficult. It is easier for the patient to hold a cup with two handles, a Manoy mug.

Fig. 15.2. The Manoy range of plastic plates and specially adapted cutlery and drinking cup for people with hand disabilities.

Some medical staff when prescribing medication do not consider how the patient is going to take it. Tablets are difficult to get out of a bottle although a jar opener can be used to turn the cap. Some chemists now put tablets into plastic pots which are easier to open. It may be better for the patient to transfer the tablets to a well-labelled 'Tupperware' container. Liquids are easier to take if they are measured in a glass rather than a spoon.

One of the most personal activities for a patient and one which is often not considered is contraception. The method of contraception is a question of personal choice, but the patient may require some advice if the method used is not satisfactory. The only mechanical method that is easy for a female patient with deformities of the hands is the intra-uterine device but this may cause heavy periods. The sheath is not easy for a man with hand deformities to manage. There is no reason why the pill should not be taken by the patient with rheumatoid arthritis. It is difficult, however, to get it out of its packaging and it is rather small to hold. Because of these difficulties it may be advisable for the partner to be responsible for contraception.

Management of household activities

Restricted movements and painful joints make household chores hard for the patient. Because of her deformities she may be slow and become easily fatigued. The therapist should work out with the patient what her priorities are, what tasks she wants to do herself and which ones either a member of her family or a Home Help should do. Heavy housework should be avoided but with the use of aids or lightweight tools and sensible planning of the day's work, most housewives should be able to cope with the day-to-day running of the home. Housework also provides useful exercise providing the patient does not become overtired and strain her joints by trying to do too much.

The patient with rheumatoid arthritis should avoid lifting heavy articles. It is therefore advisable to use lightweight pots and pans for cooking. Vegetables can be cooked in a wire chip basket inside the saucepan of water so that they can be drained by removing the basket and leaving the saucepan and water behind.

The occupational therapist should try to persuade the patient to avoid doing unnecessary work such as during food preparation. This may be hard as most housewives want to keep to their original methods of cooking. It is worthwhile, however, suggesting such ideas as boiling potatoes in their skins and buying ready cut-up meat and sliced bread. Some patients may be able to afford electrical labour-saving gadgets such as an electric mixer and electric carving knife.

Getting out to the shops and carrying purchases home may seem an impossible task. The patient should be encouraged to go out and do her own shopping if possible. If others do it for her she may become very isolated in the home. She should not carry heavy shopping bags. It is better to buy only a few things at a time and possibly carry them either in a shoulder bag or in a bag on wheels.

Doing the laundry can be made easier if heavy articles are washed in a machine or sent to the laundry. Hand-wringing should be avoided because of the damage it does to the joints of the wrist and hands. Unnecessary ironing should be discouraged. Although it may be difficult to change the habits of a lifetime some patients can be persuaded to use easy-care fabrics which do not need ironing and not to iron sheets and towels. It is advisable for the patient to sit down to iron either on a high stool or on a chair if an adjustable height ironing board is being used. A lightweight steam iron makes the actual ironing easier and less of a strain on the joints.

Light cleaning and dusting can be done by most patients but many of them insist on trying to do heavier work that could also be a safety hazard such as standing on a chair to clean the windows.

Younger patients may have the additional problem of looking after young children. This is tiring enough for an able-bodied mother but it is even worse for one who finds it painful to lift or run after the child. There is a useful booklet entitled 'The Disabled Mother' in the series *Equipment for the Disabled*.

Gardening

Gardening is a heavy activity and the patient may need advice on how to make it less taxing. Most patients do not want to, or cannot afford to, change the layout of their gardens to have raised beds. However, they may agree to have plants which are easy to look after such as roses and to have ground cover plants to cut down on the amount of weeding. The occupational therapist should suggest lightweight tools and aids for the patient to use. Sometimes it is possible to adapt the patient's own tools in the department. There are many good books on gardening for the disabled. These include *The Easy Path to Gardening* published by the Readers Digest Association in conjunction with the Disabled Living Foundation, *Gardening for the Elderly and Handicapped* by Leslie Snook, published by Pan Books and *Your Garden and Your Rheumatism* published by the Arthritis and Rheumatism Council.

The patient's emotional adjustment

The fourth aim of the occupational therapist is to help the patient to accept his disability and the limitations caused by it. When a patient is first told he has rheumatoid arthritis he is usually shocked, scared and worried about deformity. He is often in pain, which may be constant, and he may feel stiff, especially first thing in the morning. These factors can lead to depression, irritability, introspection and lack of motivation, which may result in the patient being labelled as 'difficult and uncooperative' by those around him. He may complain a great deal and demand help and attention. No doubt he has every right to behave in this way but it will hamper his interactions with others, whether they are family or the treatment team, who tend to forget that the patient may be in pain and worried about his future prospects.

The patient, however, should be informed of the effect his 'grumblings' have on others. A good book to recommend is Marie Joseph's *One Step at a Time*. In it she describes what it is like to have rheumatoid arthritis. Although quite disabled she

has not given up hope and manages to keep cheerful. She says
that although people asked her how she was she would never
give the true answer because they did not want to have a long
drawn-out description of her problems. Instead, her answer to
their questions would be that she was fine.

How can the occupational therapist help the patient firstly to
accept his disability and secondly to adjust to his role, perhaps
changed, in his family and society. Hopefully, the whole
treatment team and especially the social worker will be
involved in this aspect of treatment. Help can be given in the
hospital department to allay the fears of deformity and
disability. Not all patients with rheumatoid arthritis become
wheelchair bound and dependent on others. Many continue
life almost normally. It may be possible to arrange discussion
groups of patients, their relations and staff to talk about living
with rheumatoid arthritis. The severely disabled patient may be
worried that he will be rejected by his family because he may
become a burden. The patient may feel he is being a nuisance
when he has to ask others to do a task for him. The disabled
mother may worry about the effect her disability will have on
caring for her children. She may feel useless because she cannot
pick up her child when he cries and he may then turn to
somebody else. All these feelings can be discussed in a group
session and advice can be given either by the therapist or by
other patients who have experienced the same problems. The
relatives can also receive support from these groups even if it is
only to be assured that they are not alone in their feelings and
that help can be obtained.

A major concern, particularly among younger patients, is
the effect their illness will have on the opposite sex. Today a
great deal of importance is placed on wearing fashionable
clothes and having an attractive appearance. These patients,
because of their disability, may not be able to wear the latest
fashions. This, along with having deformities, may cause them
to worry about either not being able to attract, or no longer
being attractive to, a partner. Most human beings need to have
a loving relationship. The physical expression of this love
whether simply a caress or sexual intercourse, is important. For
a patient with deformed hands or painful joints any physical

expression may be difficult and may lead to frustration. Often a patient is reluctant to discuss his sexual problems, especially if he feels a sense of guilt due to the state of his body. Many hospital staff do not encourage discussions on sexual problems either because they do not know how to help the patient or because they assume that the disabled have no sexual urges. It is important that these patients and their partners are able to obtain guidance from trained counsellors. These counsellors discuss the couple's problems and suggest methods of overcoming them to get maximum enjoyment from sexual activity. They may advise such things as changing the position of intercourse or using sexual aids. Not all hospitals will have a trained counsellor but the treatment team should be able to answer the patient's initial questions and be able to tell him where to get more help, for instance from SPOD, a committee set up by the National Fund for Research into Crippling Diseases to research into the sexual problems of the disabled. Useful publications which may be suggested to patients include *Marriage, Sex and Arthritis* published by the Arthritis and Rheumatism Council. Dr Wendy Greengross has written an excellent book called *Entitled to Love: The Sexual and Emotional Needs of the Handicapped*. This book gives advice on how others can help the disabled to solve their problems. Some books written to help the able-bodied overcome their sexual problems are also suitable for the disabled, for instance Alex Comfort's *The Joy of Sex*.

Sometimes the emotional strain felt by the patient and his family due to the alteration in the patient's physical condition and level of dependency is too great to be tolerated. This may lead to the break-up of the family and even in some cases, divorce. The patient will need a great deal of support at this time from both hospital and community staff. If the patient is rejected by his family, permanent residential accommodation may be needed and in these instances the patient needs to be given encouragement not to give up because he no longer has a purpose in life.

RESETTLEMENT

Plans for resettlement must be made once the ADL assessment has been completed and a treatment programme involving the improvement of the patient's physical and emotional condition has been started. The therapist should consider the patient's resettlement at home, work and socially.

First of all, a home visit must be carried out. This should be an extension of the ADL assessment so that the therapist can ascertain the patient's needs in the home. This will help the therapist to plan both the treatment programme and the provision of aids and adaptations. A second home visit may be needed just before the patient is discharged to check that the aids supplied are correct and properly fitted. This visit may be carried out by the community occupational therapist, with whom the hospital occupational therapist should be in close contact.

Once the patient is discharged he becomes the responsibility of the local authority and will be visited either by a social worker or occupational therapist working in the Social Services Department.

Some patients may need to be rehoused. Careful consideration should be given when suggesting this because of the length of time it can take and also because the patient may become more isolated. If the patient has good support from relatives and friends living near him it may be better for him to stay where he is. It is hard enough for anybody to make new friends. It is even harder for a disabled person who has mobility problems. His new neighbours may avoid him because they do not know whether or not to offer help or get involved. Local authorities should provide special accommodation for the disabled. This may be in a special block for the disabled which has a warden or in a purpose-built flat or bungalow on an ordinary housing estate. The latter leads to less isolation and makes the disabled person feel he is one of the community.

There are various allowances and services available to help the disabled*. If the patient is severely disabled and requires

* Details of DHSS benefits and services for the disabled are given in Appendix 4.

constant attention at home from a relative or helper it is possible to obtain the Attendance Allowance. The disabled housewife or person who lives alone may be provided with the services of a Home Help, organized by the local authority. A government allowance is now available for disabled housewives. For the patient who is unable to cook a mid-day meal the local authority may provide 'Meals on Wheels' or may arrange for him to go to a luncheon club if he is able to get there by himself.

The occupational therapist must also consider the patient's employment. As rheumatoid arthritis has a gradual onset it may only be necessary to adapt the work at first. The exception to this is when a patient has a heavy manual job. If the patient's work has to be adapted or changed it may be possible for the occupational therapist, in conjunction with the social worker, to visit the patient's place of work and discuss with the patient and his employer what changes need to be made. These could be in the layout of the work or in the adaptation of tools.

The access to the place of employment should also be assessed and adapted if the employer agrees. Grants are available for this from the Employment Service Agency. Getting to work may pose a problem. Before invalid tricycles were phased out a patient who had a job could be supplied with a tricycle if he was capable of driving it. The tricycles have been replaced by the Mobility Allowance which is given to patients under 58 years of age who are unable to walk or who have considerable difficulty in walking. The allowance which is taxable, is supposed to cover the cost of travelling either in a private car or hired transport.

If a patient is unable to return to his former job he may be able to work part-time or to take a lighter sedentary job at the same firm. If this cannot be arranged it may be possible to start retraining the patient in the occupational therapy department and then arrange for the training to be continued at one of the Employment Resettlement Centres.

Finding new employment for the disabled is extremely difficult, especially in areas with high unemployment. It is the Disablement Resettlement Officer's (DRO) job to find employment for the disabled. Although employers are asked to have

one disabled per twenty employees this is only a recommen-
dation and is not mandatory. The DRO may be based either in
the local Employment Service Agency Office or in the hospital.

Sheltered work may be available in some areas. Remploy has
a number of factories which employ disabled workers. Some
factories have a special work area for employees who have
become disabled. The Papworth Village Settlement and the
Queen Elizabeth Foundation are two organizations that
provide residential and work facilities for the disabled. Ex-
servicemen and women may be employed at the Lord Roberts
Workshops.

If a patient is unable to find work he may be entitled to
sickness benefit, unemployment benefit and social security
benefits. The local authority may provide Day Centres for these
patients. The number of attendances depends on the patient's
needs and the availability of places. The patients may do light
industrial work or craft work and usually receive some form of
remuneration. These centres often organize social as well as
work activities.

Very often the patients' work and home situations are
considered in detail but his social and mental welfare are
forgotten. Occupational therapists were first employed in
hospitals to help patients overcome boredom. Although their
role has changed considerably since those days the therapist
should still help the severely disabled and housebound patients
to develop interests. This work need not be carried out by
trained therapists but it should be supervised by them as some
hobbies may be inadvisable. Some local authorities employ
handicraft teachers to visit patients in their homes. There are
also a number of clubs and local education classes that cater
for the disabled. One of the most popular leisure activities is
watching television. This is also a useful way of keeping the
housebound in touch with the outside world. Some televisions
have very small knobs that may need to be enlarged so that the
patient can turn them.

Loneliness is often a major problem for the patient,
especially soon after discharge from hospital where he will have
been with other people. The patient may be encouraged to join
a local club such as one of the many run by the British

Rheumatism and Arthritis Association. Some pets become good companions although they do have to be looked after. Budgerigars can be obtained free through the patient's Social Services Department contacting the Companion Trust who aim to help alleviate loneliness.

Holidays are important for the disabled whether they live alone or with their family. These can be arranged by contacting the Social Services Department. For those who prefer to arrange their own holidays the Automobile Association produces a list of hotels which provide accommodation suitable for disabled people. The Central Council for the Disabled produces town guides and also a yearly publication on holidays at home and abroad. The British Rheumatism and Arthritis Association has four hotels specially adapted for the disabled.

Many patients will not know how to obtain help. *The Directory for the Disabled: A Handbook of Information and Opportunities for the Disabled and Handicapped* compiled by Ann Darnborough and Derek Kinrade gives a guide to the main services and allowances available. It includes sections on Education, Holidays, Sport and Leisure Activities and Advisory Services.

Summary

The occupational therapist has an important part to play in the treatment of the patient with rheumatoid arthritis. She can help to prevent deformity, improve the physical condition of the patient, provide aids and suggest adaptations to make the management of his condition easier, help him to accept his disability and adjust to living in the community. The occupational therapist is only able to do this by working as a member of a treatment team.

By seeing the patient as a person with normal needs and emotions she can effectively plan and execute his rehabilitation and resettlement programme. This is of no value if the patient goes home to sit in a chair with nothing to do and nowhere to go. If resettlement is successful and the patient takes an active interest in life, the work of rehabilitation will have been worthwhile.

Appendix 1

Book List

1. *Principles of Joint Protection in Chronic Rheumatic Disease*, by Merete Brattström, MD. Translated by Mary Leonard. Printed by Studentlitteratur, Magistratsuägen 10 221 61 Lund, Sweden.
2. *Rehabilitation of the Hand*, by C. B. Wynn Parry. Published by Butterworth and Co (Publishers) Ltd, Borough Green, Sevenoaks, Kent.
3. *Coping with Disablement*, by Peggy Jay, MBAOT. Published by the Consumers Association, 14 Buckingham Street, London WC2N 6DS.
4. *Equipment for the Disabled*. Series edited at the Nuffield Orthopaedic Centre, Oxford. Published by National Fund for Research into Crippling Diseases. Orders for booklets to: Equipment for the Disabled, 2 Foredown Drive, Portslade, Sussex BN4 2BB.
5. *Your Home and Your Rheumatism*. Published by the Arthritis and Rheumatism Council, Faraday House, 8 Charing Cross Road, London WC2.
6. *How Can I/Do Others Manage with Rheumatoid Arthritis?* Prepared by the Department of Occupational Therapy of Christchurch Hospital, Christchurch, New Zealand. Published by the Arthritis and Rheumatism Foundation of New Zealand, Inc., PO Box 1801, Christchurch, New Zealand.
7. *The Easy Path to Gardening*. Published by the Readers Digest Association in conjunction with the Disabled Living Foundation. Readers Digest Association Ltd., 25 Berkeley Square, London W1.

8. *Gardening for the Elderly and Handicapped*, by Leslie Snook in the Pan Piper Small Garden Series. Published by Pan Books Ltd., Cavaye Place, London SW10 9PG.
9. *Your Garden and Your Rheumatism*. Published by the Arthritis and Rheumatism Council, Faraday House, 8 Charing Cross Road, London WC2.
10. *Designing for the Disabled,* by Selwyn Goldsmith. Published by Royal Institute of British Architects, 66 Portland Place, London W1.
11. *The Directory for the Disabled: A Handbook of Information and Opportunities for the Disabled and Handicapped.* Compiled by Ann Darnborough and Derek Kinrade. Published by Woodhead-Faulkner of Cambridge in association with the Multiple Sclerosis Society of Great Britain and Northern Ireland.
12. *One Step at a Time*, by Marie Joseph. Published by William Heinemann Ltd., 15 Queen Street, Mayfair, London W1X 5BC.
13. *Marriage, Sex and Arthritis*. Published by the Arthritis and Rheumatism Council, Faraday House, 8 Charing Cross Road, London WC2.
14. *Entitled to Love: The Sexual and Emotional Needs of the Handicapped* by Dr Wendy Greengross. Published by J. M. Dent & Sons Ltd., 33 Welbeck Street, London W1M 8LX.
15. *The Joy of Sex*, by Alex Comfort, MB, PhD. Published by Quartet Books Ltd., 27 Goodge Street, London W1P 1FD.

Appendix 2

Sources of Information and Suppliers of Aids

1. Disabled Living Foundation (DLF)
   346 Kensington High Street, London W14 8NS.
   Tel: 01 602 2491
2. Scottish Information Service for the Disabled (SISD)
   18 Claremont Crescent, Edinburgh EH7 4QD
3. Newcastle upon Tyne Council for the Disabled, Aids Centre
   M E A House, Ellison Place, Newcastle upon Tyne NE1 8XS
4. Merseyside Aids Centre
   Youens Way, off East Prescot Road, West Derby, Liverpool 14 OLR
5. Disabled Living Centre
   84 Suffolk Street, Birmingham
6. Aids Exhibition
   The Cripples Help Society, 26 Blackfriars Street, Manchester 2
7. Central Council for the Disabled Travelling Exhibition
   34 Eccleston Square, London SW1
8. Visiting Aids Centre
   The Spastic Society, 12 Park Crescent, London W1N 4EQ
9. The British Red Cross Society, Medical Aid Department
   157–159 Cavendish Road, Leicester
10. Carters Rehabilitation Equipment
    Carters (J & A) Ltd., Alfred Street, Westbury, Wiltshire

11. Surgical Medical Laboratory Manufacturing Ltd (SML)
    Head Office, Bath Place, Barnet, Herts EN5 5XE
12. Homecraft Supplies Ltd
    27 Trinity Road, London SW17 75F
13. NOMEQ (Nottingham Medical Equipment Company)
    17 Ludlow Hill Road, Melton Road, West Bridgeford,
    Nottingham NG2 6HD
14. Days Medical Aids Ltd (DMA Ltd)
    Lichard Industrial Estate, Bridgend, Mid Glamorgan
15. Self-Lift Chair Company
    Low Edge, Wychbold, Droitwich Spa, Worcestershire
16. Newton Aids Ltd
    2a Conway Street, London W1P 5HE
17. Rentool Workshops
    Royal Cornwall Hospital (City), Truro, Cornwall
18. Mecanaids Ltd
    St. Catherine Street, Gloucester GL12 2BX
19. Remploy Ltd
    415 Edgware Road, Cricklewood, London NW2 6LR
20. M. Masters and Sons Ltd
    177/184 Grange Road, London SE1 3AE
21. James Spencer & Co Ltd
    Moor Road Works, Leeds LS6 4BH
22. Kidmans Medical Aids
    40 Waterloo Road, Bedford MK40 3PG
23. F. Llewellyn & Co Ltd
    South East Princes Street, Liverpool L30 AZ2
24. Edward Doherty & Sons Ltd
    Eedee House, Charlton Road, Edmonton, London N9
25. Artificial Limb and Appliances Centre
    National Centre, Dept. of Health and Social Security
    Supply Division, DSB3B (General), Room 102, Block 1,
    Government Buildings, Warbreck Hill Road,
    Blackpool FY2 0UZ

Appendix 3

Addresses of Societies and Clubs

1. British Rheumatism and Arthritis Association, Headquarters
   1 Devonshire Place, London W1N 2BD
2. British School of Motoring Disability Training Centre
   269 Kensington High Street, London W8
3. Disabled Drivers Association
   The Hall, Ashwellthorpe, Norwich NOR 89W
4. Disabled Drivers Motor Club
   39 Templewood, London W13 8DU
5. The Central Council for the Disabled
   34 Eccleston Square, London SW1V 1PE
6. The Automobile Association, Head Office
   Fanum House, Basingstoke, Hampshire RG21 2EA
7. The Companion Trust
   Secretary, Mr J. Stewart Cook, 37 Frances Road, Windsor, Berkshire SL4 3AG
8. The British Council for Rehabilitation of the Disabled
   Tavistock House, South Tavistock Square, London WC1H 9LB
9. Help the Aged
   8 Denman Street, London W1A 2AP
10. The Disablement Income Group (DIG)
    Queens House, 180 Tottenham Court Road, London W1P 0BD
11. Greater London Association for the Disabled
    183 Queensway, London W2 5HL

12. The National Council of Social Services
    26 Bedford Square, London WC1B 3HU
13. Age Concern
    Bernard Sunley House, 60 Pitcairn Road, Mitcham,
    Surrey CR4
14. The National Association of Citizens Advice Bureaux
    26 Bedford Square, London WC1B 3HU
15. The Womens Royal Voluntary Service (WRVS)
    17 Old Park Lane, London W1Y 4AJ
16. Horder Centre for Arthritics
    Maureen Dufferin Place, Crowborough, Sussex
17. Jewish Welfare Board
    74a Charlotte Street, London W1P 2AH
18. SPOD (Sex Problems of the Disabled)
    c/o The National Fund for Research into Crippling
    Diseases, Vincent House, 1 Springfield Road, Horsham,
    Sussex
19. Family Planning Association
    27–35 Mortimer Street, London W1N 8BQ

Appendix 4

Benefits and Services

Following is a list of benefits and services provided by the DHSS for the handicapped and disabled and those caring for them in March 1978. Each case is considered individually, taking into account the patient's income and National Insurance contributions. Advice should be obtained from the hospital social worker or the local Social Security Office. Leaflets about benefits and how to claim them are available from Post Offices and Social Security Offices. The following information is taken from Leaflet FB1 Family Benefits and Pensions issued by the DHSS.

1. *Appliances and drugs* supplied by the hospital may be supplied free to some patients.
2. *Attendance Allowance.* Payable to adults and children over the age of two who are severely disabled either physically or mentally and who need a great deal of individual care and attention for at least six months. Further information in leaflet N 1205.
3. *Concessionary Fares.* Provided by the local authority, differ in every area.
4. *Day Centres.* Provided by local authority.
5. *Family Income Supplement.* Paid to families with low incomes who are in full-time work. Further information in leaflet FTS1.
6. *Home Helps.* Provided by local authority.
7. *Hospital Fares for Patients.* May be paid to a patient receiving supplementary benefit or family income supplement. Further information in leaflet H 11.

8. *Invalid Care Allowance.* Payable to people of working age who cannot work because they have to stay at home to care for a severely disabled relative. Further information in leaflet NI 212.

9. *Invalidity Benefit.* Consists of invalidity pension and invalidity allowance. This pension replaces Sickness Benefit after 28 weeks. Invalidity allowance is paid in addition to the pension to people who become chronically sick while they still have a large part of their working lives ahead of them. Further information in leaflet NI 16A.

10. *Meals on Wheels.* Hot mid-day meals are delivered to homes of people who are unable to get meals for themselves. Further information from individual local authorities.

11. *Mobility Allowance.* Paid to help severely disabled people from 5 to 55 achieve greater mobility. Payable to people who are unable or virtually unable to walk because of physical disablement. Further information in leaflet NI 211.

12. *Non-contributory Invalidity Pension.* Paid to people of working age who have been unable to work for some time and who do not qualify for full rate sickness or invalidity benefit because they do not have enough National Insurance contributions. Also payable to married women who cannot perform normal household duties. Further information in leaflets NI 210 and NI 214 (Married Women).

13. *Prescription Charges.* Some patients may be entitled to an exemption certificate or may be able to obtain a prepayment certificate. Further information in leaflets FP91/EC91, M11 and Form FP 95/EC95.

14. *Rate Rebates.* Can be claimed by owner–occupiers and tenants who are not getting supplementary benefits. Further information in leaflet 'How to pay less rates' or in Scotland, 'Rate Rebates—latest'. From local councils or Citizens Advice Bureau.

15. *Rent Rebates and Allowances.* Paid by local authority to those who have difficulty in paying full rent. Further information in leaflet 'There's Money off Rents' or in Scotland, 'Rent Rebates—read all about it'. From local councils or Citizens Advice Bureaux.

16. *Sickness Benefits.* Paid to people employed or self-employed whilst they are incapable of work due to illness or disablement. Further information in leaflet NI 16.

17. *Supplementary Benefits.* A non-contributory benefit which is payable to anyone aged 16 or over, who has left school and is not in full-time work to the extent that resources, if any, fall short of their requirements. It can supplement other State benefits or private resources. Further information in leaflets SB1, SB8, SB9, OC2 (Help with heating costs) and SL8.

18. *Help for Handicapped People.* Leaflet HB1 describes main benefits and services which are available to handicapped people.

19. *Aids for the Disabled.* Leaflet HB2 outlines the part played by the DHSS in giving information about aids and developments and supply of aids through the National Health Service and by local authorities.

Index